Praise for BUILDING A CULTURE OF RESPONSIBILITY

"I thoroughly enjoyed the book! I've never seen quite this approach taken to make effective learning come to life. The 'five pillars' concept is dynamite. It shows that while success can be simple, it's not easy. You provide an interesting roadmap for any entrepreneur, seasoned or brand new."

-- Gregory Walker, consultant, speaker, and executive

BUILDING A CULTURE OF
RESPONSIBILITY

How to Raise and Reinforce the
Five Pillars
of a Responsible Organization

MIKE WRIGHT

PHIL FISCHER

Paperback ISBN: 978-1-54393-296-6
E-book ISBN: 978-1-54393-297-3

Dedications

I dedicate this book to my wife Barbara, whose dedication and responsibility to others is a constant inspiration. – Mike Wright

This book is dedicated to my wife Marcia, without whom it would not have been possible. – Phil Fischer

ACKNOWLEDGEMENTS

In addition to E. Maximillian Paulin, the high school teacher, college guidance counselor, and guardian angel whose dedication to the well-being of others inspired the journey that that has led to this book, we'd like to acknowledge the contributions of our many colleagues, client business leaders, and comrades-in-arms who have, over the years, consistently modeled the responsibility and integrity that inspired the material in this book. They are too numerous to list, but we owe them an immense debt.

Others whose contributions we would particularly like to note are:

- Our children and grandchildren, who have given us the joy of seeing them develop to become responsible members of our society and valued contributors to our culture.

- Our many associates at The Alternative Board, who have helped us hone our skills to coach business leaders in achieving the success they envision.

- The volunteers at the Hillsboro Library Friends of Hillsboro, Oregon, who do so much good work for the benefit of those in their community.

- Our compatriots at Cara Wordsmith, Ltd. for their help in editing and proofreading this book and keeping us on point until we finished it.

- The good and talented people of Dezynamite Print & Web and Bookbaby for their invaluable help in graphic design, layout, and production.

TABLE OF CONTENTS

Read This First.. xiii

The First Pillar: Answering the Question, "Why Are We Here?".........1

The Second Pillar: Gaining Enrollment through Shared Values 26

The Third Pillar: Creating UNITY to Achieve Long-Term Success ...
Together... 44

The Fourth Pillar: Building Team Cohesion..................................... 63

The Fifth Pillar: Constant, Never-Ending Improvement 79

EPILOGUE:

What's Next? 100

Read This First

What is a Culture of Responsibility? How is it different from holding people accountable? How could answering these questions affect the success of your business?

A few years ago, Mike had the opportunity to hear a talk at a charity dinner that had a profound clarifying effect upon his outlook on success as a business leader, a parent, a grandparent and a member of society. The speaker was a man that Mike had never heard of before, and you probably haven't either: Robert Dale Maxwell. He lives in Bend, Oregon. As of this writing, he holds the honor of being America's oldest living Medal of Honor recipient.

The following citation describes what Maxwell did to earn the medal, but what Mike was more impressed with was *why* he did it … and the effect that *why* had on how we define the word "success."

On September 7, 1944, near Besancon, France, Maxwell and three other soldiers, armed only with .45 caliber automatic pistols, defended their battalion observation post against an overwhelming onslaught of flak and machine gun fire from a platoon of German infantrymen. The Germans had infiltrated the battalion's forward companies and were attacking the observation post with machine gun, machine pistol, and grenade fire at ranges as close as 10 yards. Maxwell and his unit were badly outnumbered.

Despite a hail of fire from automatic weapons and grenade launchers, Maxwell aggressively fought off advancing enemy elements. With calmness, tenacity, and fortitude, he inspired his companions to continue against long odds. When an enemy hand grenade was thrown in among his squad, he unhesitatingly hurled himself onto it, using his blanket and his unprotected body to absorb the full force of the explosion.

This sudden act of heroism permanently maimed Robert Dale Maxwell, but it saved the lives of his comrades in arms and facilitated maintenance of vital military communications during the temporary withdrawal of the battalion's forward headquarters.

As Mike thought about how this amazing true story came to happen, he wondered whether a better **understanding of Maxwell's actions on that observation post in 1944, and in the years since, could offer a clue that could help us all to lead more fulfilling personal and business lives, while at the same time positively impacting those around us.**

Another interesting story from 1944, from the other end of the chain of command, came to light as we researched the material for this book. In June of that fateful year, General Dwight D. Eisenhower had to decide whether to launch the Allied assault on France, the largest seaborne invasion in history.

The times were grim, the weather was bad, and the options were not appealing. The dilemma facing Eisenhower, Supreme Commander of the Allied forces, was this: Should he make the huge, assembled Allied force wait in position even longer than it already had, thereby reducing his chances of surprising the Germans … or should he proceed in unfavorable weather?

In the end, Eisenhower chose to take his chances with bad weather. It's notable, though, that before the invasion formally began, he drafted two very different letters for release to the press. The first letter was meant for publication if the invasion succeeded (which it did). In that letter, Eisenhower gave all the credit for the success of the mission to his subordinates and to the soldiers, sailors, and airmen who had done the fighting. The second letter was to be published in the event the Allied invasion failed. In that letter, Eisenhower took full personal responsibility for the failure of the mission.

This "tale of two letters" provided us with a valuable second point for analysis. The common factor between the five-star general and the field communication specialist was that they both displayed a strong sense of personal responsibility for their mission and their comrades in arms. Not only was this an important link in explaining each individual's action; it also demonstrated a cultural link we believe to be universal in driving positive decisions and actions.

Our mission here is to guide you, the reader, through your own journey of understanding of the kind of Responsibility both men assumed. We will do this through observations we will share and questions we will raise for your consideration.

Questions We Will Explore Together in this Book

- How much more powerful is Responsibility (that which one chooses to assume as a personal duty) than Accountability (that which someone is told to do by another)?

- How much more successful could your business be if everyone knew and embraced their own Responsibilities ... and acted unhesitatingly to fulfill them?

- How much more effective could everyone be if they took Responsibility for all interactions with each other, customers, and suppliers in accordance with shared, high company values ... and were treated in the same way in return?

- How much more satisfying and committed could all stakeholders be if they were making decisions and taking actions that everyone agreed were in the best interest of all parties?

- Isn't how people work together more important than how they work independently?

- How much more effective and efficient is it to lead and manage high performing *teams* ... rather than individuals?

- How much better could your business perform if each individual within it were committed to continually learning and improving so that the team could become the very best in its field ... with the support of all key stakeholders?

Your answers to these and other questions will help you understand the Culture of Responsibility we have seen in action, and chosen to write about here. Our goal is to help you and everyone in your company understand this Culture of Responsibility and implement it successfully within your organization. The examples we will share are not dictates about how this must be done. They are illustrations of how other leaders have implemented these principles, as we have observed the Culture of Responsibility taking hold over many years, in many organizations and in many walks of life. The achievements we share here are important not because they are extraordinary or unattainable, but because they are not beyond the ability of most businesses to implement. They illustrate the remarkable universal power of Responsibility. We believe anybody can do this, in any walk of life.

We have selected both civilian and military examples to best illustrate, magnify, and clarify the universal principles of what we have come to call the Five Pillars of Responsibility. Make no mistake: This is a book about success for people and teams of all kinds. There is, of course, a big difference between the soldier's environment and the working environment in which civilians operate, where the worst-case scenario is losing some money or a job! Even so, we believe that the examples we have chosen for the later chapters of this book are all potentially instructive for individuals and teams, regardless of the realm in which they operate.

A KEY QUESTION

The first question that arose for us was: *Is the Culture of Responsibility or the level of responsibility assumed by Robert Dale Maxwell impossible in the modern workplace?*

Our answer, based on personal experience and observation, is an emphatic "No." We say this because:

- We have seen dramatic growth in teams that adopted these principles and have brought a much fuller sense of personal commitment to the workplace, regardless of the age of the companies or experience level of the employees.

- We have seen employers and employees take personal responsibility and build deeper, more rewarding workplace relationships.

- We know the roots of Robert Dale Maxwell's actions and Dwight D. Eisenhower's were planted well before his action on that battlefield. In his situation, as well as in other examples we will present, decisions and actions were driven by a series of experiences and distinctions that can be, and should be, incorporated into any meaningful concept of "success" in the workplace. (By the way, Maxwell's experience on the field of battle hasn't stopped him from making great contributions to the education of youth and others in his community to this day!)

A CULTURE OF RESPONSIBILITY IS POSSIBLE

Changing people's behavior or an organization's culture doesn't come about overnight. This requires support, coaching and reinforcement. But it definitely does happen. We know, because we've experienced it happening on many occasions. Every time it happens, it happens around a single, powerful word, the same word that was behind the decisions of Robert Dale Maxwell and Dwight D. Eisenhower: *Responsibility.*

By the way: Maxwell's decision to throw himself on a live grenade was not unique in situation or time in history. In preparing this book we found many Medal of Honor recipients who made similar instantaneous heroic decisions, putting their own lives on the line in order to defend the lives of their comrades. Again, this doesn't happen by accident. Interestingly, when you read interviews with the soldiers who managed to survive this kind of event – and of course not all of them did – you tend to see the same answer surfacing over and over again in response to the inevitable question, "Why did you do that?" It usually sounds something like this: *"I just happened to be the person who was closest to where the danger was; the other guys would have done the same thing for the team if they'd been closest."* That extraordinary response describes a kind of *total team cohesion* that we call UNITY. And yes, it is profoundly relevant to the workplace. (We discuss UNITY in depth in The Third Pillar.)

In researching and writing this book we discovered time and again that the principles or pillars of Responsibility, such as UNITY, are a vital force supporting all meaningful business and societal successes. We have selected a few of these examples to serve as illustrations in this book.

WHAT WE MEAN BY "RESPONSIBILITY" – AND WHY IT MATTERS

There are several keys for developing a full understanding the concept of Responsibility. Among the most important is the concept of a link between one's ability to assume personal responsibility and one's personal growth and development throughout life. One of the major sources of inspiration for this book came from a statement by the Center for Parenting

Education. It reads as follows: **"Being responsible is a key to children's success both in school and in the larger world when they grow up."**

Effective leaders build on this principle by accepting that **Accountability is not the same as Responsibility.** By putting forth such a principle, we are challenging the common preconception that teams are best managed by holding them strictly "accountable." This is because we define **accountable,** as most people do, to mean: **The state of having been *assigned by someone else to* carry out an action or to act in a specific way.** By contrast, when we use the word "**Responsible**," we mean: **The state of having been *personally chosen* to carry out an action or to act in an agreed-upon way.** A manager can make someone accountable for something … but Responsibility only comes when that person makes a *conscious choice* to take on the obligation as a personal commitment.

Most teams and organizations are low on Responsibility level and high on external accountability. And most managers, unfortunately, don't know the difference.

On many teams, hardly anyone takes personal Responsibility for achieving the team's goals. Often, the sense of obligation and commitment comes from someone at the top, or someone outside the team, pasting obligations onto the surface of the employee's world. The duty does not penetrate that surface to effect who the employees ARE as human beings.

Robert Dale Maxwell, and the countless others before and since who have offered his level of sacrifice, made a very different personal choice: a choice to be RESPONSIBLE for the team with which he felt Unity. And yes, any other member of the team would have done precisely the same for Maxwell. (This mutual trust is critical to UNITY.) Maxwell saw no difference between the team's survival and his own. For him, the two were exactly the same. *This can and does happen in the workplace – and in the chapters that follow, we'll show you how it can happen.*

Responsibility creates UNITY

As you'll see in Pillar Three, UNITY is the fusion of the individual and the team. It is an extraordinary level of personal, mutual commitment. It is a way of living as much as it is a way of working. And it is rooted in the personal Responsibility that comes from within and can't possibly be imposed from the outside. We'll share more about UNITY in later portions of the book.

TRUE LEADERSHIP

Some businesspeople who find themselves in positions of authority think primarily in terms of accountability – meaning they build their day around the act of giving orders, and making other people accountable. They seek power and control. When there is failure, and there often is, they hold others accountable for it.

Other business leaders take a very different approach. They assume personal responsibility for the pursuit of a worthy goal or mission; they enroll others in that mission and act responsibly toward them; and they adopt a distinctive, two-tiered strategy for handling the team's outcomes. If the outcome is good, they give the credit to other team members. If the outcome is disappointing, or even painful, they assume personal responsibility for the team's failure – as Eisenhower was ready to do.

That's true leadership. And please note that it is rooted in Responsibility. First and foremost, we leaders must learn to be responsible ourselves. Without that, nothing great is possible.

Assuming personal Responsibility may not always be our first instinct. Yet it is non-negotiable if we want a team that functions at the highest level.

Only when we have begun this process of assuming personal responsibility can we begin to get a clearer understanding of the concept of the pathway to true mutual Responsibility.

WHY THIS BOOK?

There are a lot of good books on leadership out there, and a lot of good ideas to process. Why should you read this book or try to implement the ideas within it?

The best answer we can give you is a simple one: We've worked with a lot of companies over the years, and we've seen the same basic principle play out over and over again: *Good ideas come and go … but transforming the culture of your organization to embrace Responsibility is the only thing we've seen that delivers sustainable positive change.*

That's what this book is all about, and it's what the true stories we will be sharing here illustrate: How to launch, sustain, and make permanent a powerful cultural transformation that will make Responsibility a daily reality for everyone in your organization.

If you are a leader aiming to achieve something special in the workplace, you should know that you're only going to get the best results if you create a Culture of Responsibility that is based on personal Responsibility ... from the bottom to the top.

A Culture of Responsibility drives the powerful personal choices that make team-based Responsibility possible. This is the same culture that led Robert Dale Maxwell to see himself and his team as precisely the same thing and that led General Eisenhower to assume personal responsibility for the results of his (huge!) team's efforts. If that's the kind of team you want to lead, and be part of, you've come to the right place. We will help to guide your efforts to make a Culture of Responsibility a reality for you and your organization by raising and reinforcing the **Five Pillars** that support that culture.

They are:

The First Pillar: Answering the Question, "Why Are We Here?"

- o Set the vision. And live it!

The Second Pillar: Gaining Enrollment through Shared Values.

- o Win buy-in on core principles

The Third Pillar: Creating UNITY to Achieve Long-Term Success ... Together

- o Inspire, nurture, and sustain UNITY

The Fourth Pillar: Building Team Cohesion

- o Create and support a "one for all and all for one" approach to the workplace

The Fifth Pillar: Constant, Never-Ending Improvement

- o Set a course for ongoing excellence on both the personal and the organizational level

Responsibility is more than a catchword, or a program you implement, or a poster you pin up in the break room. It is a way of living life that drives people's decisions and actions on the best business teams, and supports them as they do the right thing for their customers, for their teammates, and for their companies.

If this sounds like what you want for yourself and your organization, let's begin.

THE FIRST PILLAR:

Answering the Question, "Why Are We Here?"

Set the vision. And live it!

"Vision without action is merely a dream.
Action without vision just passes the time.
Vision with action can change the world."

Joel A. Barker, futurist, author, lecturer, and filmmaker

It was July the first, 1965. Mike's first day at West Point.

You start that first day at the United States Military Academy as one kind of person, and you come out of it on the other side as someone entirely different. It's a day designed to change your life forever, and for the better – as it did for Mike.

Wherever you go that day, you're running or marching as a group. Your posture, your movement, your dress, and your speech patterns become uniform. You and your classmates end up, at the conclusion of a very long day indeed, marching in formation to Trophy Point, overlooking the Hudson River near Battle Monument, which memorializes those who gave their lives in service in the Civil War.

How does Responsibility (that which you choose to assume as a personal duty) contrast with Accountability (that which someone else tells you to do, and holds you accountable for doing)?

At this majestic point, so steeped in the history of the nation, the swearing in ceremony of the Class of 1969 was to take place. Before that occurred, though, the new cadets were to listen to a recording of the address that General Douglas MacArthur had delivered to the new cadets of the Class of 1966, as they entered the Corps at this same place three years earlier. Mike still remembers many of those words. In particular, he recalls hearing General MacArthur's voice ringing out with the following words:

Duty, Honor, Country: Those three hallowed words reverently dictate what you ought to be, what you can be, what you will be. They are your rallying points: to build courage when courage seems to fail; to regain faith when there seems to be little cause for faith; to create hope when hope becomes forlorn.

Unhappily, I possess neither that eloquence of diction, that poetry of imagination, nor that brilliance of metaphor to tell you all that they mean. The unbelievers will say they are but words, but a slogan, but a flamboyant phrase. Every pedant, every demagogue, every cynic, every hypocrite, every troublemaker, and I am sorry to say, some others of an entirely different character, will try to downgrade them even to the extent of mockery and ridicule.

2

But these are some of the things they do: They build your basic character. They mold you for your future roles as the custodians of the nation's defense. They make you strong enough to know when you are weak, and brave enough to face yourself when you are afraid. They teach you to be proud and unbending in honest failure, but humble and gentle in success; not to substitute words for actions, not to seek the path of comfort, but to face the stress and spur of difficulty and challenge; to learn to stand up in the storm but to have compassion on those who fall; to master yourself before you seek to master others; to have a heart that is clean, a goal that is high; to learn to laugh, yet never forget how to weep; to reach into the future yet never neglect the past; to be serious yet never to take yourself too seriously; to be modest so that you will remember the simplicity of true greatness, the open mind of true wisdom, the meekness of true strength. They give you a temper of the will, a quality of the imagination, a vigor of the emotions, a freshness of the deep springs of life, a temperamental predominance of courage over timidity, of an appetite for adventure over love of ease. They create in your heart the sense of wonder, the unfailing hope of what next, and the joy and inspiration of life. They teach you in this way to be an officer and a gentleman.

The speech was a transformative one, coming as it did at the end of a transformative day. It clarified for Mike, and for all the cadets in his class, the reason they had come to West Point. That reason lay in the intersection of the words, Duty, Honor, and Country.

At the conclusion of the playback of General MacArthur's remarks, Mike and the other cadets assumed personal responsibility to uphold the values of Duty, Honor, and Country as military officers in training. Here is what they raised their hands and swore:

> "I, _____, do solemnly swear (or affirm) that I will support and defend the Constitution of the United States against all enemies, foreign and domestic; that I will bear true faith and allegiance to the same; that I take this obligation freely, without any mental reservation or purpose of evasion; and that I will well and faithfully execute the duties of the office on which I am about to enter, so help me God."

Notice the emphasis on personal choice in those words. That's the key. That's the sign that the vision is a truly compelling one: People make a conscious decision to support it once it's been set; they embrace their Responsibility on a personal level. And they become a different kind of person, a better person, as a result of that choice.

By the way: It should be noted that before asking the New Cadets to take Responsibility, General MacArthur affirmed his personal belief that they could and would be successful. That's leadership in action.

On that day, Mike began the journey toward a whole new way of life: a life as an officer and a gentleman. A life of personal honor and Responsible service to others. A truly fulfilling life. He would later study a line by the poet Richard Lovelace that would guide him on that journey:

*I could not love thee, dear, so much, loved I not
honor more.*

Mike has encountered many situations that tested his ability
to apply the ideals he took to heart on that warm July day, but
there were none so memorable or pivotal as what happened at
the strategically important Air Defense Guided Missile battery
he took command of in South Korea in 1973.

A 26-year-old Captain who had graduated from West Point
just four years earlier, Mike had been assigned to the battery
because it had been having some significant problems. His first
impression was that the team he was responsible for leading
– which comprised 100 US personnel and 20 South Korean
augmentation forces – had many good people who were not
performing at the level of which they were capable.

The people who reported to Mike seemed to him to be working
in a disconnected manner. Without teamwork and synchroni-
zation, they were going through the moves. The morale was
flat, confidence was lacking, and positive energy was low. He
felt that, in a challenging situation, this unit might struggle to
rise to the occasion, and he wondered what would be the best
way to handle this problem.

As it happened, Mike found out that a solution would be
needed sooner than expected – or desired. The battery got hit
with an Operational Readiness Evaluation, and it failed mis-
erably. It was judged to be unable to accomplish its mission as
the "hot battery."

A FAILURE THAT SET UP SUCCESS

Of the four batteries in the battalion, at any given time one of them, the "hot battery," had the responsibility of being ready to fire missiles within minutes to repel an enemy aircraft attack, and give other US and South Korean resources time to respond. If a surprise attack came from North Korea, China, or anywhere else, the hot battery was the first line of defense. It was critical that vulnerable allied aircraft not be exposed while they were still on the ground. The next two batteries had time to come up and join the fight. The fourth battery was always in deep maintenance.

As the hot battery, Mike's battery was subject to an Operational Readiness Evaluation (ORE) at any time of the day or night. Early on the fourth evening of the vulnerability period, the inspection team arrived on site and sounded the siren to final arm the missiles and be ready engage the enemy. The crew on duty jumped to action to come to "Battle Stations".

Within less than 45 minutes, the Group Inspectors had declared the battery incapable of performing all aspects of its critical mission, and the standby battery had to assume hot status. The silence after the Group Inspectors left was deafening.

This was serious. Mike's team had to correct the problem in short order. Whenever a battery failed (and in effect, the battalion failed that test), it had to correct whatever problems the test identified and pass a re-evaluation within one month. Mike and his team had just a few weeks to prepare. This was quite a task. He had not had much time to adjust to the people under his command, or they to him. He had never faced a challenge quite like this, but he knew it was his responsibility to take it on. He had to come up with a plan to rectify the situation and ensure that that level of performance wouldn't happen again.

All the battery's officers and senior non-commissioned officers (NCOs) assembled for a meeting. As it turned out, that meeting would transform not just the battery he commanded, but the trajectory of Mike's life and the lives of many others at the meeting. It began a process of collaboration that served as an example of what can be accomplished by a Team that is working together, a Team where every member takes responsibility for a common goal and shared values. In such an environment, the Team ultimately imbues each member with a sense of confidence and excitement about what can be accomplished while working with others.

TAKING RESPONSIBILITY

The message Mike began the meeting with was a simple one: It was his personal responsibility to find a way to fix what had happened. And he would need everyone's help in doing so.

He didn't complain. He didn't assign blame or look for scapegoats. He didn't issue ultimatums. He assumed personal responsibility for what had just happened – that, after all, is part of the leader's job, and perhaps the most important part – and he told the team he was going to be relying on them, because he knew that a turnaround was going to be impossible without their help.

> The Leader sets the vision, and must assume personal responsibility for poor performance of the team. If there is a failure, it's because the leader has not yet established an environment where people can succeed. If that's not there, the leader is the one responsible for finding out what the problem is.

It's worth noting here that at the time of this meeting, Mike was 26 years old and had spent less than four years as an officer, and the senior NCOs he was meeting with were in their thirties to early forties. These men had four to six times the length in service that Mike did. This situation is quite common within a military structure, wherein the officers are accountable … but the NCOS have the experience and the insight that serve as the foundation of the team's achievement. In this case, the battery was supported by a warrant officer responsible for overseeing the maintenance of the equipment. Mike needed this warrant officer's help. The man had over two decades of experience. If you added up the experience of all the commissioned officers in the room, including Mike, it wouldn't have equaled this man's years of experience! He had a name plate on his desk that said "THEY." When he asked someone why they had done something, and they responded that "They told me to," he would point to the nameplate and state, "No I didn't!"

A NEW POSSIBILITY

After Mike opened the conversation by assuming personal responsibility for what had just happened, the team got down to business.

One of the first things everyone in the room had to acknowledge was that they each had to get back up to the level of being ready to perform as the hot battery. In addition to needing to prepare for the all-important re-test, they still had the responsibility for initial response in case of an attack from hostile forces. They were literally on the front line … and had to improve. Mike got the team engaged by presenting a new possibility. He painted a picture of a way forward that appealed, not to his position and authority as commanding officer, not to his rank on the org chart, but to the honor and professionalism and self-image of the people gathered in the room.

The possibility Mike presented was this: What if they not only passed the upcoming test, but performed at a level of proficiency that the inspectors had never seen before?

What if their turnaround was so powerful, so complete, so dramatic, that the inspectors not only gave them high marks, but asked how the turnaround had been achieved. What if they did so well that other batteries would benefit from what Mike's team had learned and accomplished and find out how they had attained that level of mastery?

The men around the table (yes, they were all men) bought into that possibility – including, critically, the warrant officer. Mike's vision was the new possibility they created. What he elucidated was their new mission – not simply passing the test, but setting a new standard that inspired the inspectors and led them to ask, "How did you do that?" That was what the battery was all about now. And it was energizing.

During that meeting, the team decided that the only way to recover was to go above and beyond, and to reclaim the honor and respect that everyone in the room knew had been compromised.

Once the team was aligned around that goal, Mike and the team focused on the responsibilities of each of the battery's three main areas.

- The fire team that goes down to the launchers and arms the missiles.

- The fire control crew – the people in the control van who run engagement, identify targets, and lock on, and fire missiles. (Of course, they don't fire missiles during a test, but they do have to show they're prepared to do so.)

- Maintenance – the people who take care of repairs and run the radar and power generation operations.

In the past, officers had not asked NCOs about better ways of doing things. The NCOs had not pursued better procedures, based on a belief that leaders would not be supportive or even interested if they did. This, however, was a new situation. The team discussed the many ramifications of poor communications, which included steady declines in response times and overall performance. From this day forward, officers in the battery listened more effectively. They started asking better questions, getting better answers, and supporting constructive action. The NCOs and the crews began exploring better ways of doing their jobs.

The new approach, the new vision, and the new challenge before the team had a galvanizing effect. The battery had never been in a situation where everyone had a task to perform beyond "just getting a passing score" – and a reason to perform at the *highest* possible level. Now they did. Each of them were now being asked to buy into the vision of not just passing the test, but of reclaiming their rightful place of honor by taking responsibility for achieving at an *optimal* – not just an acceptable – level. The executive officer and platoon leaders took responsibility for coordinating activities and insuring that the crews had what they needed to implement their improvements.

The daily routine of the battery changed. No longer were people trying to simply get through the day. They were striving for something that was important to them, on both a personal and a team level. A shift in mindset had occurred.

By the time the team got to the readiness re-evaluation, it wasn't something anyone was afraid of or uncertain about. Each and every member of the team was looking forward to that test. Each and every member of the team wanted to show how well everyone was performing within the organization.

The re-inspection was a triumph. All areas of the battery scored at very high levels and in a manner of drill that the evaluators had not seen before. The evaluators asked if they could recommend that representatives from other batteries observe the drills and learn more about how the teams had developed and implemented their best practices.

Mike made sure the *team* – not him – received full credit for the victory.

THE REWARD

In delivering a glowing out-briefing, the evaluation team reinforced the impact of what the battery had accomplished for each member of the battery team. It was a team win and a collection of individual wins. The win was made possible by people who took individual responsibility and supported each other as a single unit.

The resulting confidence in their ability to perform carried through to the October of that year, when US forces were called up to Defense Readiness Condition DEFCON 3, a serious ratcheting up of tension. A brief explanation: Defense Readiness Condition is the alert state. Only DEFCON 1 (meaning nuclear war is imminent) and DEFCON 2 (the next step below imminent nuclear war, under which armed forces must be ready to deploy in no more than six hours) represent higher stages of threat. At that time, North Korean MIG aircraft began high speed probes of the DMZ. The battery crews were locking on and requesting permission to fire should the North Korean planes penetrate South Korean airspace. Everyone on the team knew they were up to the task. Every crew member *wanted* to be among those on duty when duty called. The energy was high. There was no doubt of their ability to perform.

Although targets were locked on and engagement authorization was pending, the MIGs changed course. Fortunately, and no missiles were fired.

The battery had come a long way – from simply getting through the day to *wanting* to be on the front lines at the moment of greatest peril!

> "The moment you take responsibility for everything in your life is the moment you can change anything in your life." – Hal Elrod, author and motivational speaker

TAKE OWNERSHIP!

The first pillar is all about taking ownership. It's all about assuming responsibility. In the military environment, the reward may be, and should be, connected to acclaim and promotion, but more importantly, it is about the personal fulfillment that comes from having protected and served others through your actions. In the business world, the rewards can also include financial rewards, but those financial rewards may not be as important as people think. In the end, both worlds operate on rewards that connect to the individual's self-esteem and ability to connect to others. The strong leader should be sure to recognize and reinforce these feelings in the individual and the group. The sense of accomplishment and the feeling of being valued by the team will have a much more lasting and powerful impact on future performance than monetary rewards … but when coupled together they have a strong multiplying effect. Even a significant financial reward, when not tied to positive action or a sense of being part of the team, will not have a sustainable positive impact on performance levels.

The big question is a simple one: WHY? As in "Why am I coming to work each day?" Once people have a big enough WHY – a WHY that matters to them on a personal level – they're more likely to take action in a way that makes a difference to the team. That was certainly the case with Mike's battery.

A compelling vision gives people a good answer to question, "Why are we here?" In the case of Mike's battery, the answer to that question was all about reclaiming the honor and respect that went with performing their mission of protecting our forces and our allies at the highest possible level. What better guiding purpose! They deserved all the respect they received. They had taken Responsibility … and diligently done the work for which they were Responsible.

TWO TRUE STORIES

Consider the following situations, and ask yourself whether they are similar to anything you have experienced.

Recently, a client of ours who runs a dog kennel was sharing her concerns about the difficulty of finding good talent, talent she could feel great about hiring. Her company's turnover was high and had been high for some time. She complained that for many of her prospective new hires, there seemed to be no sense of personal commitment to the job being applied for – or indeed to any job. "I want to interview people who really love taking care of dogs," she said, "people who love being part of a team that does that. That's what motivates me when I get up in the morning: being part of a team that connects with animals and their owners and makes their lives better. But all too often, when I interview entry-level applicants, what I find is that they seem to view *all* work as a detour from what they really want to do with their lives, if they have even thought about that. They don't approach their identity as a team member in the work-place as a major priority. They want to get work *done,* so they can go back to thinking about what really matters to them."

When she said this, we had to admit that we had run into our fair share of similar behavior.

When asked if they had accepted the responsibilities of this or any job, she was unsure.

A friend of ours shared his experience helping a relative who had recently been let go from his job with a nonprofit organization after a two-year stint there. In the weeks following his termination, the man who had been let go was approaching his job search campaign with a certain sense of entitlement – a feeling that the world somehow owed him a living, and that the decision makers he was reaching out to somehow had an obligation to put the goal of meeting his employment objectives at the top of their to-do lists. When they didn't, the man became angry and depressed, and called our friend once a week or so to get sympathy. "I do want to support him," our friend told us, "but I find I have to balance the support I give him with a message from the real world: No one is under any obligation to give you anything. You have to *give* something first, to start with, you have to give people the impression that you're grateful for their time and for the opportunity to learn about them, and about their organizations. You must be persistent, patient and keep following up. You can't assume people will make your problems their priority unless you show that *you* are interested in *them*."

Think of what these two situations have in common. How do they relate to Responsibility and to success? For us, each story illustrates a situation where the individual has not yet bought into a compelling personal or organizational vision that extends beyond mere self-interest. This is the essential first step when it comes to building a team whose foundation is Responsibility. This transition is not always easy. But it is always the first step!

LINKING THE INDIVIDUAL AND THE TEAM

Note that people *must* buy into the vision as individuals for the team to perform at an exemplary level. If they don't, they won't perform at a top level. Self-interest is basic human nature, but the best leadership aligns that self-interest to team or company goals to achieve greater returns for everyone. This requires that they understand the personal visions and goals of each person -- and align them with the team's and organization's goals and visions. This cannot be achieved by *dictating* team goals to the employee, nor can it be achieved by blaming them if they fall short. Understanding the varying levels of responsibility (which are strikingly parallel to Maslow's famous Hierarchy of Needs) means understanding where the *individual is in terms of security, belonging, and confidence,* and the strength of his or her current personal commitments. It also means being committed to and behaving in accordance with your values and priorities to inspire the team member to expand that level of commitment.

MASLOW'S HIERARCHY OF NEEDS

This is what sets the best leaders apart. They know everything starts with the personal responsibility of the leader. They hold themselves Responsible to the individuals' well-being and look ceaselessly for ways to get individuals to buy-in, and contribute fully to, the accomplishments of the team. They know these accomplishments must matter to each and every member the team and give them a sense of being part of something bigger than themselves. This plays out in what we call the Hierarchy of Cultural Responsibility. Notice that the leader's role in setting the vision is the foundation of this hierarchy.

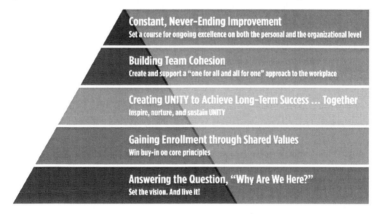

THE HIERARCHY OF CULTURAL RESPONSIBILITY

Linking the individual to the team by means of a shared vision is not the same as stepping in to "show them how it's done." Notice that it was *not* Mike's job to take over the individual responsibilities of people on his team. He couldn't possibly have done that. If he had tried, he most certainly would have failed, and his team would have too. All too often, when a leader tries to go it alone or overextends him/her self, the results are negative. Feeling left out, people watch passively while waiting to be told what to do. Their sense of responsibility wanes and they lose confidence in the leader and the entire organization.

Interestingly, failure or adversity can be a catalyst that unites people, giving them a sense of shared purpose and the energy needed to achieve much higher results. The right leader may be able to inspire the team after a major setback simply by asking them to respond and demonstrating full confidence in them. This was certainly the case in Mike's battery. In a business setting it might look like this: You lose a big account you had for years – and you focus on determining why you lost that customer. As a result, you gain a better understanding of that customer and many other customers. Your team may renew their processes and/or attitudes. Now, more engaged and confident and with a sudden sense of purpose, they go out and win more business from the competitors that took the account from you.

Occasionally you will encounter that rare person who is resistant or even hostile to the team's effort. In this case, it may be time to rethink that person's role within the team. The common expression is that "a chain is only as strong as its weakest link." Our experience, though, is that disruption to norms and order makes all of the links weaker. This causes a loss of productivity throughout the organization. Very often, when such a person is removed, the response from the rest of the team will be along the lines of, "Why did you wait so long? That person was holding us back and destroying team cohesion!" What the team can accomplish with one less member is sometimes amazing.

Linking the Individual and the Team: FEI

Setting the vision is a critical organizational priority. Embracing it is a critical individual decision. Mike's story illustrates the importance of the organizational vision perspective. An early passage in Phil's career illuminates the personal perspective.

Early in his career, Phil worked for FEI Company. Much later on, this company was sold for several billion dollars. When Phil worked for it, however, as a young marketing and sales manager, it was a tiny specialized technology firm, employing about twenty people.

By all accounts Phil was doing a fine job. Sales were growing, market visibility was increasing, his team was performing, and he was liked and respected by both co-workers and customers. However, his immediate supervisor, the company's COO, informed Phil that despite his successes, his growth prospects in the company would be limited by virtue of Phil's failure to effectively articulate and communicate his VISION for his team and the company.

Over and over, Phil kept hearing variations on a persistent question from his supervisor. *What was his vision for the company?*

Specifically: Where did he think the company was going to be in five years? And how did his role and his team's role need to change to support the growth that was planned for the company?

All of this talk of vision was, initially, a little confusing to Phil. He'd been hired to do a job. He was fulfilling the requirements of that job. He was hitting all the organizational and performance targets that had been set out for him. What did it matter where he thought the company or anyone else was headed in five years? He was there to do to a job – build a sales team from scratch and launch an ambitious new product line targeted to a market that knew little or nothing about this small Oregon company – and he was doing it. Wasn't that all that mattered?

He didn't have a clear vision beyond that, and he really didn't know what to say when he was asked about it. Yet the question wouldn't go away.

It's important to note here that the answer to the COO's question didn't come overnight to Phil.

The answer came, as it often does, over time. And it came about, as it often does, as the result of consistent reinforcement of the company vision from the senior company leaders.

Phil started paying more attention to words from company's founder and Chairman, a highly-regarded physicist who had developed the technology that was the basis for all of the company's products and its strategic plan. The Chairman had a strong and clear vision for the company. He wanted FEI to take the technology he had created – which had powerful capabilities to analyze and modify materials in what would eventually become the field of nano-technology – into practical tools for industries ranging from electronics and semiconductors to biotechnology, advanced materials, health sciences, and energy. This vision extended beyond the company itself; it had the potential to contribute to technology breakthroughs that could change people's lives for the better, transform whole industries, and leave a positive mark on the world.

Month after month and year after year, the physicist shared that message with the stakeholders in the business; shareholders, customers, vendors, employees, and anyone else he felt could benefit or contribute to achieving that vision.

There was no "light bulb" moment for Phil. This was a slow accumulation of long-term priorities, reinforced over time by a visionary communicator. That's one of the leader's most important jobs, by the way – reinforcing his or her vision. It's not enough to lay out the vision once. It's not even enough to lay out the vision a dozen times, or a hundred times. This is a permanent part of the job description, and possibly the most important part!

There came a point when Phil knew that he understood and shared the physicist's vision. He now understood what his supervisor had been asking about, and, just as important, what his answer was. He knew why he was showing up for work each morning … not just to earn a paycheck, but to create a sales and marketing team that could facilitate deployment of this breakthrough technology on a global level, bring radical positive change to multiple industries, and improve people's lives.

Phil's whole approach to work changed because his why had changed. Powered by that new why, he launched a number of new team-focused initiatives – whereas before he had been focused primarily on his own responsibilities and the performance of individual salespeople. (For instance, he created weekly communication sessions where sales professionals operating in different countries could share insights, strategies, and updates that supported the team.)

Phil now had a guiding purpose beyond simply performing his duties. He had evolved gradually from the position of not having a guiding purpose to the position of taking personal responsibility for his part of the company vision. Only a persistent, ongoing reinforcement of the company vision from a persuasive leader made that transition possible.

ASK NOT ...

By definition, a great guiding purpose inspires RESPONSIBILITY. Consider John F. Kennedy's stirring challenge to the nation in 1961: "Ask not what your country can do for you, but what you can do for your country." When people take responsibility for their contributions to something larger than themselves, the results are better for everyone. As a manager, your job is to accept responsibility first, get the people who report to you to the point where they not only understand but BUY INTO your vision, and then inspire them to make the team goal a reality in their own lives. That's what Kennedy was talking about. He challenged each and every citizen in the country to ask, "What can I do to move from a 'me-only' mindset to a 'me-as-a-key-part-of-the-team' mindset?"

One final point before we move on. It's important to note that this principle is vitally important, whether your organization consists of 5, 50, 5000, or 500,000 people. The tools and resources you have access to will, of course, vary, but every organization can and should create and communicate its guiding vision and core values, connect all people and teams to them, and ensure that they have the resources to both implement them and live by them every day.

Set the Vision – and Live It!

THE TAKEAWAYS: PILLAR ONE

Success is a lifelong journey, and Pillar One is the first critical step on that journey. It requires a change of outlook.

When we first come into the world, someone else is responsible for almost everything in our lives: feeding us, protecting us, taking care of our every need. We slowly begin to learn to take responsibility for ourselves. Cleaning up, brushing our teeth, getting good grades, doing chores, or taking on a job to get money for things we want are all examples of this.

Eventually, there come points in our lives when we choose to take responsibility for others – for people, for teams, and even for principles that support our important relationships. The important thing is learning to *feel* personally responsible for your own life. That means identifying *who* you are responsible to … what you are responsible *for* … and connecting with others who will help you on your journey. Ideally, we begin to feel satisfaction of doing our chores or our job, because in addition to those things we were doing for ourselves we were also doing things for others.

To begin building a Culture of Responsibility the leader must:

- Assume personal responsibility for the poor performance of the team. If there is a failure, it's because the leader has not developed the individual responsibility in the people or has built his or her team incorrectly.

- Be responsible for establishing an environment where people can succeed. If that's not there, the leader is responsible for finding the barriers and removing them.

- Create the vision that paints a picture of the future that inspires each and every individual.

- Establish effective two-way communication within the organization.

- Develop experienced managers who have everything they need to execute in accordance with the norms of the organization, who train their team members, equip them, and structure their work, while continually connecting them to the larger vision and the path to greater success.

- Ensure that every individual clearly understands the vision for the future and his or her responsibilities for team success, and (this is key) *accepts those responsibilities as their guiding purpose.*

THE KEY QUESTIONS FOR PILLAR ONE

- What is the vision for this organization?

- Who (by name) is ultimately personally responsible for the success or failure of this organization and of every initiative it pursues? (Identify one person.)

- Do people know these individuals? Do they know what each of them has been entrusted with personally taking Responsibility for in support of the whole?

- Is there a better way of communicating in the future?

Answer the questions above in writing. Once you've done that, consider sharing your responses with members of a peer group who can help you to identify the best follow-up questions ... and continue your organization's journey toward full Responsibility Culture.

THE SECOND PILLAR:
Gaining Enrollment through Shared Values

Win buy-in on core principles.

"When your values are clear to you, making decisions becomes much easier."

Roy Disney, longtime senior executive for the Walt Disney Company

Mutual trust in clear shared values is the lubricant that keeps great teams and organizations moving forward. There are any number of ways people choose to define that elusive word "values." Our favorite definition is a simple one. *Values are how we operate around here when no one is looking.* A great example of this would be Joe Berger, the General Manager of the Hybrid Component Operation of Tektronix (HCO), who sent powerful values messages to the entire team ... simply by acting in accordance with *his* values. On one occasion, he communicated the importance of organizational cleanliness in a moment, without words. Walking down the hall while discussing a business issue with Mike, he casually leaned down picked up a piece of stray litter and placed it in a trash receptacle. He did this without comment or distraction, eloquently sending the message to the few people who saw it: "This is how we do things here. We're all responsible for pitching in to keep things in order, regardless of job title." It worked!

What would it mean to the success of your business if your people all embraced and understood their Responsibilities … and acted unhesitatingly to fulfill them?

While Joe never made comments to draw attention to what *he* did, he always showed authentic personal appreciation for anyone in the organization who demonstrated the organization's values.

An individual's values may be spoken or unspoken, accidental or a matter of conscious choice. Very often, leaders find that the individual team members are operating under different, or even competing and incompatible, value sets. This is a failure of enrollment.

Organizational values may best emerge as a consequence of **an ongoing dialogue**, a dialogue that is continuously driven by the leader. We believe it's best for everyone when an organization's values are clearly elucidated and chosen by the leader – as a direct result of his or her personal experience and, specifically, the personal experience with the team.

The notion of conversation is an important one that will recur throughout this chapter. Productive values are not something pasted on from outside. They're not dictated from the top down. They're built into the enterprise, and constantly reinforced, by means of an ongoing discussion about what drives a person to show up for work, day after day, week after week, month after month, and year after year. When we fail to continually communicate and reinforce these values by our own actions as leaders, we lose alignment within our team, and the team loses respect for the leadership.

Values are the way we think and act, both individually and as a group, without prompting. The best organizational values are those the members of the team have

* seen modeled by top leaders;

* assumed conscious personal responsibility for upholding;

* learned to follow naturally;

* reinforced through constant action;

* used to set accurate expectations about how teammates will think and act.

Acting in accordance with a certain value you hold yourself responsible for should feel natural to you; it should not be an effort, and it should not feel like speaking a foreign language by silently translating to or from your native language before you speak. This spontaneous action, even when it's quite simple (as Joe's was) is itself a kind of ongoing conversation.

Notice that this ongoing conversation is a matter of sharing a personal response to changing situations, adapting to challenges, and performing in a highly synchronized manner with the team. Remember: *Values are all about action.* We emphasize this point because, too often, managers mistake values for a single "vision statement" or "mission statement" sentence that needs to be recited – but never implemented.

Ronald Reagan's Five Core Values

In his 1985 State of the Union address, Ronald Reagan explicitly appealed to five core values that had already been points of constant, vigorous internal discussion within his Administrations for the past four years: *faith, freedom, family, work, and neighborhood.*

Reagan said:

> *Now, there's another great heritage to speak of this evening. Of all the changes that have swept America the past four years, none brings greater promise than our rediscovery of the values of* **faith, freedom, family, work, and neighborhood.** *We see signs of renewal in increased attendance in places of worship; renewed optimism and faith in our future; love of country rediscovered by our young, who are leading the way. We've rediscovered that work is good in and of itself, that it ennobles us to create and contribute no matter how seemingly humble our jobs. We've seen a powerful new current from an old and honorable tradition—American generosity. From thousands answering Peace Corps appeals to help boost food production in Africa, to millions volunteering time, corporations adopting schools, and communities pulling together to help the neediest among us at home, we have refound our values.*

An understanding of the Reagan presidency is impossible without an understanding of these five values: faith, freedom, family, work, and neighborhood. They were the stars by which he navigated the ship of state. Those five deceptively simple-sounding ideas were actually the principles by which Reagan managed his White House. Notice that we used the word "managed" – which is not to be mistaken for the word "micromanaged."

Reagan hired, engaged with, evoked responsibility from, and empowered people whom he knew he could trust to uphold those five core values. If you couldn't share his values, you couldn't work for him. It was that simple. He managed by holding good discussions about those values … and by making the final decisions on that tiny minority of issues that could not possibly have been resolved at a lower level. Everything else, he left to people whom he knew shared his values … and whom he trusted implicitly.

Reagan was not under any illusion that it was his duty to make decisions *for* the people who reported to him. His job, he knew, was to demand the best possible decisions *of* the people who worked for him, based on those five shared values. As leader of the free world, he was willing to stand behind their decisions. If the decisions worked out, that was all well and good. If there were problems, he would lead the team as the problems were sorted out. Usually there weren't problems, though. Reagan's was an extremely effective presidency; most historians now agree on that. Virtually every respected list places him in the top half of the American pantheon of great leaders, and most place his administration in the top ten. Consider that the first three names on that list are always Lincoln, Washington, and Franklin Roosevelt, and you have some sense of the level of accomplishment of the Reagan White House. *That historic accomplishment was driven by Reagan's ongoing discussions of shared values.*

Colin Powell, who took part in dozens of those conversations, and who served as Reagan's national security advisor, tells a fascinating story that illustrates this values-driven dimension of Reagan's leadership. In his book *It Worked for Me*, Powell recounts a time when he was dealing with a seemingly insoluble conflict between the State Department and the Defense Department. In Reagan's office, Colin went on and on about the rivalry between the two departments, about the implications of the unresolved issues, and about all the potential difficulties of any available course of action. As he spoke, though, Powell noticed that the President's attention appeared to be elsewhere.

Powell kept on trying to summarize the problem he wanted the Chief Executive to solve. But he still seemed distracted. Powell kept talking. Reagan kept on looking elsewhere. Eventually, Powell realized that the President was staring out the window at something. That's when Reagan said: "Colin, Colin, the squirrels just came and got the nuts I put out there this morning."

That, Powell realized, was as much of an answer to his pressing problem as he was going to get from the President.

Powell retreated to his office, pondered the situation, and came to realize that he had just been paid a huge compliment by the man in the Oval Office. In essence, Reagan was saying: "I hired you because I trusted you to share in the values that are important to me, and to America. I trust you to make the right decision. What you're describing is your problem. If it reaches the point where it's my problem, come back and let me know. In the meantime – make the best decision you possibly can, based on our shared values."

That's what great leaders do. Identify, set, and reinforce the values ... empower the team ... and stand back.

DIRECT PERSONAL RESPONSIBILITY

The most effective, most transformative organizational values are those that are deeply rooted in the direct personal responsibility of the organization's LEADER to the TEAM.

Unfortunately, many owners, managers, and leaders get this equation backwards. They expect responsibility from the team first, and forget (or overlook) the reality that the leader's responsibility to the team must always come first. *Otherwise there are no shared values at all, no matter what memos you send out, no matter what slogans you hang on the wall.*

This kind of personal responsibility is absolutely essential. It's modeled daily from the top, and it's what makes the difference between the "values" that show up in mission statements and on the posters of break rooms, without ever affecting the actions of most employees – and the shared values that positively impact the team's ability to unite behind a goal, work collaboratively, and achieve breakthrough results. This kind of personal responsibility transforms the organization and commands greater and greater chunks of the market. It makes a tangible competitive difference for companies, day after day – because people are making decisions about where to go next while holding compasses that agree on which direction is North. That's the power of shared values.

> Our values should reflect our responsibility to provide what is expected and relied upon to each other and to our customers.

Values rooted in personal responsibility from the leader to the team are *actual* values. By contrast, values rooted in words and phrases that people memorize, but don't live by, are *fake* values, and they don't lead to any meaningful positive changes in team cohesion and performance. In fact, they often do more harm than good.

Values in Action: Charlie Lake, Warne Scope Mounts

We can think of no better example of the kind of responsibility we're talking about – the kind that gives everyone agreement on which direction is North – than the story of Charlie Lake, owner for twelve years of Warne Scope Mounts, a design and innovation leader in the field of firearms optical mounting solutions. (Note: The company was sold in 2012, and it continues to grow its market share under the new ownership; the events described here took place before the company's sale.)

Charlie's example is a powerful one because of his habitual emphasis on the ongoing conversation about organizational values. As a leader, you do need to know the values that drive your team, but you also have to understand that identifying these values and reinforcing them over time is a collaborative process with the team. It's an ongoing series of conversations – like Reagan's ongoing conversation about faith, freedom, family, work, and neighborhood. This conversation is a process that plays out over time and strengthens the team. It's rooted in action and affects the specific values the team embraces. It's not something pasted on from outside. This conversation always begins when the leader demonstrates personal responsibility to the team. The members of the team are in turn responsible to the organization, buying into both its goals and values with full force. The result is an attitudinal change, up and down the organization, which moves from, "I am responsible for so and so" to "We are all responsible for delivering X, Y, and Z to our customers."

The leader's most important job is to identify and constantly reinforce the CORE ORGANIZATIONAL VALUES that drive this transition. Even coming out of challenging times, it is the people who take responsibility for identifying and supporting key organizational values who become stronger and who make their organizations stronger. Charlie is a great example of such a person. He found himself in a highly competitive industry, pressured by Chinese manufacturers who offered one and only one reason to buy their product: they could offer it to the consumer cheaper. That was the reality Charlie, a veteran of the high-tech industry, faced. He could have wasted time, effort, and energy complaining about the overseas competition. He could have found a way to externalize the problem. But he didn't. He assumed responsibility for **leading the conversation about values,** about the kind of company he wanted to create. He asked a critical question: **"How are we going to get a whole lot better than they could possibly ever get?"**

That's a great question, one that's part of the values conversation, and one we encourage you to ask yourself and your own team. For Charlie, the answer to that question boiled down to four constantly-reinforced, constantly-examined, constantly implemented ideas:

- Quality (as defined by customers and partners)

- Responsiveness / Velocity

- Ideation / innovation

- Engagement / Teamwork (with employees, customers, and partners)

FOUR OVERLAPPING VALUES

Understand that those four ideas, which inevitably overlapped in their daily execution, didn't just emerge automatically. They weren't posters that Charlie ordered online and hung up on the wall of the coffee room. They were the unique result of an ongoing *conversation* involving Charlie, his customers, and the members of his team. The reality of any meaningful list of organizational values that actually gets implemented, actually drives behavior, is that the list becomes clearer over time, and particularly after one has faced, and overcome, serious challenges.

Notice that the values Charlie used to develop, challenge, and inspire his team are *not necessarily the values you should use to develop, challenge, and inspire your team.* In fact, it would be remarkable if they were. Your Core Organizational Values must arise out of your own conversations with your own team.

We don't want to leave you with the idea that these four ideas constitute a "finished" or "authoritative" list. It's in the nature of a conversation to continue, and any good list of organizational values – Charlie's included – is subject to revision, change, and expansion. Having said that, and having acknowledged that these are not the *only* four values that shaped Charlie's company, we can move on to take a closer look at how they worked together to deliver a massive positive impact.

Charlie's unyielding commitment to the organizational value of Quality, for instance, connects to the related value of

Engagement/Teamwork. Both values came out of his years in the high-tech field, where tight, focused, connected work teams and ongoing feedback from user groups can and do combine to make a huge competitive difference. Because we had the honor of working with Charlie, we know that his faith in the power of engagement and teamwork in setting new quality standards extended to his vendors and customers as well, connecting and sharing, without fear of criticism, ideas and insights that might help make things better became part of the Warne Scope Mount team culture. And Charlie's brand of inclusive Engagement, intensely focused on Quality, made some truly remarkable things possible.

Charlie made sure that Engagement/Teamwork extended simultaneously in multiple directions: to customers, to employees, and to business allies. Our favorite example of this has to do with a major trade show that Warne Scope Mounts was scheduled to take part in. This was an annual event. Normally, Charlie and a few marketing people showed up and manned the booth. During one of the meetings we attended, though, Charlie shared an exciting idea: What if a cross-section of the entire company attended the event?

Charlie not only arranged for administrative and support people (who had nothing to do with marketing) to take part in the convention. He also trained them to use the scope mounts their company sold and the weapons these went on, so that they should show prospective customers, in person and from direct experience, exactly how easy to use it was and how much more accurate it made the weapon.

This emphasis on direct Engagement had a number of positive effects. Perhaps most noticeably, it led to huge, excited crowds at the company's booth. People simply weren't used to interacting with non-marketing people who had personal insights to share on why they loved what they did for a living and why they loved creating (and showing off) a quality product. So, the people at Charlie's booth stood out. Secondly, it made the team members feel appreciated and valued. And third, it gave everyone in the organization – not just the people assigned to the conference, but the entire organization – a much stronger sense of personal ownership of the company's overall mission of satisfying the customer base. They had a personal reason for what they were doing at work each day.

Charlie was equally focused on Engaging with customers, of course – a habit that intersected with the values of quality and Ideation/Innovation. A constant, ongoing discussion with end users, and a willingness to listen to their ideas on how to make the product better, was another critical organizational value.

This is one of those areas where Charlie seized on an opportunity to leverage a major competitive advantage against foreign competitors. It might have been true that Chinese manufacturers could create and market a *cheaper* product for the American market – but it seemed unlikely that they could do a better job of listening to American gun owners about what they wanted in their experience with the product. Charlie resolved to do that listening, and he motivated everyone in his organization to adopt the same attitude, no matter what his or her job description was.

There were other areas where Ideation/Innovation paid off. Some scope manufacturers, for instance, made their own scope mounts. Charlie and his team showed them a new possibility: Warne could provide them with better mounts for their scopes with more functionality and greater ease of use – at a competitive price. Warne offered a scope mount that was significantly easier to use, and significantly more accurate, than those offered by foreign competitors. The new product was a hit.

By the way: This relentless focus on Ideation, on generating and sharing good ideas from customers (and everyone else) eventually led to being forced to raise prices – to distinguish Warne's products from those of the competition, whose costs were increasing due to rising prices from foreign suppliers who were offering products of inferior Quality. This strategic choice led to a higher recognized value in the marketplace, higher market share, and much higher profits.

Ideation means looking at something familiar from a different point of view. It's an essential part of the Quality conversation with customers – but of course, it's not limited to customer discussions. The value of Ideation – which literally means "the process of forming and relating ideas" – is really central to the success story we were privileged to be part of at Warne Scope Mounts. It's what led Charlie and his marketing, engineering, and manufacturing teams to their target. They ended up serving a whole new market segment: scope manufacturers. (Previously, the company had sold almost exclusively through distribution channels that sold to individual rifle owners wanting to buy upgraded replacement mounts.) This breakthrough took the company's performance to a whole new level.

Ideation is coming up with the idea. Innovation is the process of *translating* an idea into goods or services that create value or for which customers will pay. In Charlie's case, promoting and supporting the ongoing innovation conversation took many forms – so many, in fact, that we can't list them all here.

One example that does stand out, though, was the application of this concept to internal manufacturing and supply chain processes, in the ongoing examination Charlie and his people made into finding and removing inefficiencies from the manufacturing process. This connects to both the value of Quality and the value of Velocity. By ensuring that everyone in the organization, and particularly the engineers, lived and understood the productive, time-sensitive value of innovation (as opposed to, say, the less-than-productive, time-wasting value of proving that you were right about something, or scoring political points against another work group), Charlie and his team were able to significantly reduce both time commitments and manufacturing costs.

Improved collaboration played a big part in the Velocity value. To explain: Transferring a product from design to prototyping to preproduction to production is often a drawn-out process, requiring extensive communications and interdepartmental back-and-forth. By bringing engineers closely together with production people in a process of "protoduction," the path to full production was made much smoother. This, in turn, positively impacted the team's Velocity … and, ultimately, its responsiveness in delivering Quality products.

Another example of the Velocity value in action had to do with efficiency of capital. Warne timed their payment for materials, their collections from customers, and their manufacturing lead times to allow them to collect payments from customers for finished products *before* they paid suppliers for the materials with which they were made. This provided an even greater financial benefit over competitors that used offshore suppliers.

Notice that Velocity has to do, not just with speed, but with direction. Charlie didn't just want his team members to focus on accomplishing tasks quickly. You can move quickly and make a lot of mistakes along the way if you focus simply on increasing your speed. Charlie wanted people to accelerate effectively toward the attainment of *certain goals* – goals that made sense for the customers, for the company, and for the individual team members.

This particular value, Velocity, really resonated with everyone who worked at Warne Scope Mounts. It's a great example that shows how leadership can harness the power of language in establishing and sustaining Critical Organizational Values for a unique work team. Instead of simply reminding employees to show up on time (or putting up a poster about punctuality), Charlie made it his job to discuss, define, model, and engage with people on the value of Velocity. That was far more effective.

THE NEVER-ENDING CONVERSATION

Charlie assumed personal responsibility for reinforcing the four values – Quality, Responsiveness/Velocity, Ideation/ Innovation, and Engagement/Teamwork – in the team culture, in an ongoing, never-ending conversation. Again, these values didn't come to him overnight. They emerged over time, and became clearer once he and his team had dealt with a little adversity. **Once they became clear, they defined both the individual team member and the team as a whole – and they also helped to identify, for everyone, (not just management), which people on the staff didn't fit in and needed to find somewhere else to work.** That's the power of Core Organizational Values that the leader actually *lives*. They make it very, very easy to identify who should – and shouldn't – be on the team. When someone consistently refuses to live by the value of, say, Velocity, everyone notices!

We were privileged to see Charlie's ongoing values conversation in action. Whenever team members came to Charlie with a problem, it became a teaching moment for him, one that usually connected to one of the four values we've shared with you in this chapter. Through dialogue with team members and a clear focus on Quality, Responsiveness/Velocity, Ideation/Innovation, and Engagement/Teamwork, the problem was not only solved, it was often solved by the team member in a way that everyone involved could understand. Charlie's consistent ability to focus on these values, and his personal example in living them, made the people who came to him for help better able to handle future challenges.

> Values aren't buses... They're not supposed to get you anywhere. They're supposed to define who you are." – Jennifer Crusie, bestselling novelist

Clarify Your Values!

THE TAKEAWAYS: PILLAR TWO

Our values should reflect our responsibility to provide what is expected and relied upon to each other and to our customers. As leaders, we certainly need to know the values that drive the team, but we also have to understand that identifying these values and reinforcing them over time is a collaborative process with the team, an ongoing series of conversations that we must lead, first and foremost, with our own actions.

- The most effective, most transformative organizational values are those that are deeply rooted in the direct personal responsibility of the organization's leader … and instilled in the team through both words and actions.

- Values are the way we think and act, both individually and as a group, without prompting. The best organizational values are those the members of the team have:

  o seen modeled by top leaders;

  o consciously assumed personal responsibility for upholding;

  o learned to follow naturally;

  o reinforced through constant action;

  o used to set accurate expectations about how teammates will think and act.

THE KEY QUESTIONS FOR PILLAR TWO

What positive, transformative values can you currently identify among your organization's top performers? (For instance: Inclusive Engagement/Teamwork.)

What values, if incorporated into your organization's culture, would enable you to deliver something to your customers that your most daunting competitor couldn't possibly deliver?

How will you lead the conversation about those values?

How will you model them on a personal level?

Answer the questions above in writing. Once you've done that, consider sharing your responses with members of a peer group who can help you to identify the best follow-up questions ... and continue your organization's journey toward full Responsibility Culture.

THE THIRD PILLAR:

Creating UNITY to Achieve Long-Term Success ... Together

Inspire, nurture, and sustain UNITY.

"Great teams do not hold back with one another. They are unafraid to air their dirty laundry. They admit their mistakes, their weaknesses, and their concerns without fear of reprisal."

Patrick Lencioni, author and management lecturer

How much more effective could every one of your people be if they took personal Responsibility for interacting with each other, customers, and suppliers in accordance with the same high company values ... and were confident that they would be treated in the same way?

The third pillar of responsibility is all about sharing a commitment to the long-term success of two or more engaged teams or organizations, a commitment that goes beyond the borders of the individuals or teams working on a specific immediate goal or project. This is a critical principle, one that we call UNITY.

You'll be reading a lot about UNITY in this chapter. UNITY strengthens the entirety of both organizations through the bond of working together to achieve an important, mutually accepted outcome. The result goes beyond any specific win-win situation, and creates a long-term platform for collaboration.

> UNITY happens when a powerful shared mission unites two or more groups and effectively turns them into one.

UNITY means something well beyond "being on the same page," as the current management jargon is content to put it. Plenty of people who are "on the same page" in terms of project objectives or task assignments have starkly different visions of what the larger goals are – different reasons, if you will, for showing up for work. We call that state of affairs INTERSECTION – and it's not the same thing as UNITY. Consider these two graphics, which illustrate the difference between INTERSECTION and UNITY.

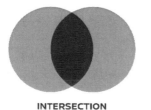
INTERSECTION

UNITY

The figure on the left represents INTERSECTION. As you can see, there is an obvious overlap between the two groups – a zone where they can be said to be "on the same page." But overlap is not enough. It's possible, indeed likely, that the groups in question may each have an accurate understanding of the project, its main objective, its timelines, and so on. *However, a shared long-term goal, and a mutual understanding of each other's vision is not driving the project.* There will be conflicting priorities, conflicting agendas, and disagreements about "how we work around here." There is no shared unity of purpose.

The figure on the right represents UNITY. In this situation, the two teams have literally combined to form a single team with complementary visions and a shared long-term goal. Both teams appeal to that goal to determine "how we work around here" – both in theory and in practice.

What's fascinating, and what many managers don't realize, is that those two circles – each with a different center of gravity in the illustration on the left, each with the same center of gravity in the illustration on the right – can represent work teams from multiple organizations. So, while it's true that, with good leadership and consistent implementation of the principles discussed in this book, we can get our internal departments such as sales, manufacturing, and accounting to move from INTERSECTION to UNITY … it's also true (and just as important) that we can get one of our own teams and an outside team, such as a vendor, to move from INTERSECTION to UNITY.

IKE DEMOTES AN OFFICER

A great example from history of a Leader successfully moving a team from INTERSECTION to UNITY would be the joint Allied command that coordinated the massive assault on Normandy during World War II – also known as D-Day. Supreme Commander Dwight D. Eisenhower – later, of course, elected President of the United States – inherited a team that was in a state of INTERSECTION. There were British officers, and there were American officers. Ike was responsible for getting the British and the Americans to cooperate in such a way as to coordinate the largest marine assault in the history of human warfare. This was not easy in the early weeks of the mission's planning phases, however, as there was constant infighting and backbiting between the two groups.

Eisenhower made it clear that there was only one group reporting to him as they planned the great mission that would eventually liberate Europe: *officers*. There were to be no cabals, no rivalries, no political games that pitted the Americans against the British, or vice versa. From Eisenhower's perspective, national alliances, as a practical matter, simply ceased to exist in terms of the working relationships of the senior Allied command. A great example of just how seriously Eisenhower took this principle can be found in the following true story. Having heard, and confirmed through discussions with eyewitnesses, that an American officer had insulted a British officer by calling him a "son of a bitch," Ike gave an order demoting the American officer and exiling him from the command team. When the British officer involved in the discussion heard about this, he appealed to Eisenhower to reverse his decision and reinstate the officer in question. In his letter, the British officer insisted that moments of tension like the one he had experienced from the American officer were to be expected, and should be forgiven. Would the general reconsider? Ike did a little more digging and forwarded a concise, but powerful, written reply: "I am informed that he called you a *British* son of a bitch. That is quite different. My decision stands."

The incident illustrates how totally committed Eisenhower was to absolute UNITY among the members of his senior command. Mere INTERSECTION was not enough. The two groups had to have the functional equivalent of a single identity, and anything threatening that was subject to the highest scrutiny and quick, impossible-to-misinterpret action. Imagine the effect that decision of Ike's had on future discussions between American and British officers. They knew at that point, surely, that if they weren't focusing on the shared mission of defeating Hitler, rather than on irrelevancies like their cultural or national differences, they no longer had a place on the team.

> *"That's how a real team works. You help the people around you, and everybody's better off for it. The crazy thing is that most of those guys (who supported us) wanted to be astronauts, too, but they never saw it as a competition. We were on the same team, where you want everyone around you to be as successful as possible, because in some way or another, their success will become your success. It's good karma - what goes around comes around."*
>
> Mike Massimino, space shuttle astronaut

REWRITING IBM'S RFP

Here's a practical business example of the difference between INTERSECTION and UNITY. In the early 1990's, a Tektronix components manufacturing division we discussed in Pillar Two, Hybrid Component Operation (HCO), recognized for their excellence in producing high bandwidth components, received a Request for Proposal from IBM – the global information technology juggernaut. One of the HCO engineers reviewed the proposal and told his team leader, "You know, they've designed the part they're telling us that they want us to manufacture ... but I can see a way we can redesign this part in a way that would enable us to consistently produce more reliable parts much more efficiently. By doing this we can make a greater profit while saving IBM a lot of money over the long term ... and providing their customers with better-quality products."

HCO's team could have simply given IBM what it said it wanted. It could have followed the RFP to the letter and shelved any reference to the idea the engineer came up with. That would have been an example of INTERSECTION. In that case, there would have been no powerful long-term force uniting the two teams and organizations.

On the other hand, if they had gone to IBM with a proposal that contained the design concept the engineer had proposed, a design that was somewhat more expensive in the short term than simply fulfilling the specs of the RFP would have been ... if the HCO's team had explained that the stronger long-term option was a better, lower-cost solution that improved IBM's bottom line and supported its goal of delivering quality products to consumers ... that would have been an example of UNITY.

And that is exactly what happened: UNITY. IBM accepted the idea, revised its RFP, and went with the new design. In doing so, the two companies developed a trusting ongoing collaborative relationship, and laid the groundwork for a major success. An interesting side note: Part of what made this UNITY possible was IBM's proprietary PROFS network, which provided what we would today call instant messaging and e-mail services between the collaborating parties in this alliance. These were major strategic weapons in the early 1990s – and an essential collaborative tool in creating the new component!

"Purpose is why we do what we do. It is the missing element in most organizations. Almost any organization can tell you it's mission and vision, and a few can tell you their values, but I think those are almost worthless in their ability to drive the daily behavior of employees. Most of your employees can't remember your elaborate mission and vision, and even if they could, they can't see themselves in it. Purpose, on the other hand, is a powerful guide to daily behavior, because purpose lives in the hearts and minds of those that serve the purpose.... How you get to purpose is critical if you want it to be truly shared. Don't take a walk in the woods with your senior leaders and some high-priced consultant some weekend and appear on a Monday morning to anoint your purpose from on high. That will be about as exciting to your employees as your mission statement. Engage your employees in dialogue and let the purpose arise from the relationship you have with them, the relationship they have with each other, and the relationship they have with your customers and suppliers."

Bret Simmons, Associate Professor of Management, University of Nevada at Reno

MOVING BEYOND FINGER-POINTING

Years ago, when Mike worked at Tektronix, he received word of an urgent call from a major client of the company's HCO division: Trillium Semiconductor.

The people at Trillium were complaining that Tektronix had sent them a shipment with a great number of faulty parts. These were extremely expensive, and extremely sensitive, components used in semiconductor manufacturing processes based on complex integrated circuit designs. Mike talked to his own team members, and each and every one of them confirmed personally that the components in question had been tested and had left Tektronix as 100% fully functional. In other words, the problem was something that had happened after the shipment left Tektronix.

Mike's team shared this information with Trillium, but the response that followed was not a positive one. The people at Trillium still insisted that they should be sent good parts.

A round of recrimination and finger-pointing began, with representatives of the two companies stating the facts from their perspective based on their goals and objectives. They were debating a classic, endlessly entertaining question: "Who Messed Up?" Each side was doing what people most companies do, protecting their interests as they saw them and proving that "the other guy" had made a mistake. No one was troubleshooting the actual problem.

Mike and Joe Berger, the General Manager, finally ended the game by scheduling a face-to-face meeting with the senior management of Trillium. During that meeting, they moved past the goal of proving that one side or the other was "wrong," and persuaded the top people at Trillium to buy into shared goals. HCO would manufacture replacement parts to get Trillium going, and they would have one of their production managers travel with the new parts to the Trillium facility. She would review the Trillium processes for receiving the parts and delivering them to production.

Notice how different this approach was from digging in their heels and destroying the relationship. Joe and Mike's position could have been: "I stand by my people – if they say the parts tested at 100% when they left our building, then that's the reality we need to accept. Somebody on your side is damaging the parts." This, however, would only have exacerbated an already tense situation. Alternatively, he could have said, "If your people tell me the parts are damaged, then we must have damaged them, so we're going to send replacement parts." This response would only have continued the cycle – because it wouldn't have gotten anyone any closer to the answer to the only question that mattered: "What is causing the parts to fail?"

It was a good thing that those first two (easy) responses were rejected and that Mike and Joe chose to press the more difficult one. That decision led to a breakthrough. Trillium would allow Tektronix to serve as an on-site consultant, so the two companies could figure out what, exactly, was going on? Trillium's senior management said yes – and from that moment forward, the two companies were aligned in a state of UNITY. They were both committed to the goal of **supporting Trillium's production process.**

That's a very different goal than proving that you're right or proving that you're willing to do whatever the customer says … before all the facts are in. Fortunately, it was a goal that all sides could agree on.

After a single day spent in the Trillium facility, the Tektronix representative shared her findings. These findings solved the problem – and a much deeper sense of mission between the two companies was made possible.

The parts were indeed functional, on arrival at the Trillium facility, improper handling procedures were causing them to be destroyed. Tiny surges of static electricity were killing the unprotected components once they were unpackaged. Regardless of who was at "fault," the outcome left each party stronger.

By inserting their own production person into the client's production environment, by merging the two teams to focus on the objective, HCO's people were able to get to the bottom of what was really happening. Instead of pointing fingers, they discovered the root cause of a major problem, and helped Trillium understand a challenge in their reception and manufacturing processes. And they focused on a goal that made sense to both sides: **supporting the Trillium production line.**

By moving beyond the blame game, Tektronix was able to move beyond being a supplier of components. They became a partner in the Trillium manufacturing process, a role that expanded over time and led to a much closer business relationship.

"An important decision I made was to resist playing the Blame Game. The day I realized that I am in charge of how I will approach problems in my life, that things will turn out better or worse because of me and nobody else, that was the day I knew I would be a happier and healthier person. And that was the day I knew I could truly build a life that matters."

Steve Goodier, author and speaker

UNITY ON THE SALES TEAM

Back in the early 1990's, Phil was tasked with creating a new comp plan for the international sales force he led. Creating a compensation plan that keeps all the members of the team happy is difficult enough when you're working with a team whose members are all based in a single country ... but it's a uniquely challenging undertaking when the team members serve markets in different countries, and rarely if ever occupy the same building.

Phil wanted a plan that would encourage his people to work together seamlessly. He wanted a system that would inspire and support a team mentality that had sometimes been lacking. And he wanted a system everyone could understand ... and feel good about.

It took some doing. After a series of in-depth discussions with all the team members, he came up with a system that still rewarded team members for their individual sales, just as the previous system had done, but that also introduced a modest but measurable team reward as well. In other words, the individual received a bonus based on team performance.

In addition, Phil made a point of scheduling regular conference calls that involved all the salespeople, regardless of the country in which each salesperson worked. This, too, fostered a sense of share purpose: The reason for the call was to strategize on the goal of *making more money for the team ... and at the same time for the company as a whole.* The real team, after all, is the entire company.

These two changes made the individual salespeople more likely to approach questions from a team perspective – to share insights, tips, experiences, and contacts in pursuit of the team reward. In short, the new approach made it easier for the sales team to operate in the zone of UNITY, to function as a true team, rather than as a collection of independent entities.

Not all salespeople on Phil's team were "natural" team players. Most were classic "hunters," used to working on their own. This was not a phenomenon unique to Phil's organization; most of the sales leaders we've met have had to deal with some version of this challenge. But even hunters can find a reason to cooperate – if doing so helps them to bring down a large target.

In Phil's case, the reason to cooperate was simple and direct: there was a greater chance of winning a team bonus by working with someone else to secure a major account than there was of landing the major account all on one's own. Many of the opportunities on the team's radar screen were simply too large for one person to close independently.

It's worth noting here that these weekly phone conferences were not *just* attended by salespeople. In support of the CEO's guiding vision for the company, Phil arranged for other key people to sit in from time to time. The CEO himself would take part in the discussions when his schedule permitted, sharing insights and observations that kept discussions on track and promoted a sense of common purpose. The head of R&D occasionally sat in on the meetings as well, and his participation carried two important advantages. First, he was able to share his perspective when he felt the sales team was on the verge of promising something that the technical team couldn't deliver. Second, he got a first-hand look at the real-world pressures the sales team was facing in the marketplace, and he came away with a new respect for their responsibilities and their achievements.

A common theme of the weekly discussions was "everything connects." The individual members of the sales team not only got a clearer sense of what their counterparts in other countries were going through, and how they could work together more effectively. They also began looking more closely at how their current projects affected other teams and people in the company. A sense of shared mission across both national and departmental lines emerged. The members of the sales team began to think, not just of their own interests, but of the intersection between the customer's long-term interests and the long-term interests of their own company.

Working together, meeting more often than they had before, and united by the possibility of securing an ever-larger reward for the sales team while supporting the growth of the whole company, Phil's team managed to develop significantly more business relationships with large multinationals. These were huge businesses with multiple operations that crossed national lines. In some cases, the salespeople were working in partnership with one another to create offers that appealed to multiple decision-making networks within the same company. In others, they created proposals for individuals with independent decision-making authority on the purchases. But they were always communicating with each other about their experiences, and they were always sharing insights and phone numbers, which was quite an accomplishment. The result was a greater level of success for the sales team as a whole, broader market share, more major accounts, and a deeper sense of team cohesion. The new approach got salespeople to look beyond their own territory and encouraged them to collaborate more constructively in moving deals forward. That's the power of UNITY.

HELPING THE CLIENT COMPANY .... BY HELPING ITS INDIVIDUAL EMPLOYEES

Most people who sell insurance policies to companies don't bother creating individual consulting relationships with each of the individual employees the policy covers. But that's not the case with Joel Biernat of Benefit Design Group, who takes such a personalized approach to client service that he regards each and every one of the employees covered by his customer's policy as worthy of time, attention, and individual consulting when it comes to setting up the right plan and receiving benefits.

That's a major investment of resources, but here's why he does it: Joel is convinced that the very best way to serve his customer (the company) is to focus on the shared goal of creating a special kind of workplace where people are cared for, satisfied, happy about their careers, engaged, and motivated to contribute at a high level.

That's UNION, because it's the same goal that company leadership has endorsed and the same goal that each individual employee he coaches buys into. Joel knows that by coaching and supporting claims on an individual level, he's supporting his customer – the company – by making each individual employee feel attended to as he or she navigates the often-confusing world of plan selection and claims processing. Employees think, "Wow. This guy is spending time with me, helping me as I figure this out. Ownership must think I'm important, because they've brought a person in here specifically to help me with the paperwork."

Make no mistake: Joel is not just helping people file paperwork. He's helping the company deliver on the goal of having happier, more satisfied, more productive employees who stick around for longer periods of time. He's helping the company far, far more than someone who simply "sells an insurance policy" – and then walks away.

UNITY IN ACTION

Being committed to a powerful goal that extends across traditional boundaries leads to some amazing examples of commitment and dedication. Here's one of our favorite (true) stories of that kind of commitment.

Ed Guzman heads up a data network support company called Cogent IT, which is based in Beaverton, Oregon. One Saturday evening, Ed was at home watching the nightly news when he saw a story come on about a four-alarm fire in downtown Portland. He thought he recognized something familiar on the screen. Leaning in closer to the TV, he confirmed that he was looking at something familiar: the building in which one of his best clients had his offices.

Without thinking twice, Ed picked up the phone and phoned the client. He told him that his building was on fire – and that he would meet him at 8:00 AM the next day (a Sunday!) so they could start planning what they were going to do to get his employees networked, and working at full capacity, on Monday morning. That's exactly what they did. By Sunday afternoon, they were prepared for the employees to begin the new work week.

Obviously, Ed was totally committed to the goal his client shared – of keeping his team up and running with the latest and best available network connections. That's what real UNITY looks like in action.

Make UNITY Your Daily Reality!

THE TAKEAWAYS: PILLAR THREE

UNITY enables the highest level of team success!

UNITY only happens when a powerful shared mission unites two or more groups and effectively turns them into one.

- When you reach the state of UNITY, you're basically functioning as one unit on a day to day basis – regardless of the formal organizational boundaries. Unity can be achieved between different departments, different countries, or different companies if team members all accept responsibility to consistently act in support of shared goals.

- Blame-assignment and finger-pointing are far more common than Unity in most workplaces, both internally and externally. Although Unity can lead to superior results, many Responsible leaders do not understand and don't actively encourage it.

- When a team member starts playing the blame game (by, for instance, reinforcing a sense of rivalry and disagreement between Accounting and Sales), it's time for a deeper discussion about UNITY.

- Include people from "different worlds" or with different perspectives on your teams, to make everyone part of an expanded world.

- Hold regular discussions among participants with radically different responsibilities to facilitate UNITY.

- Facilitate real-time forums for discussing the changing dynamics of current projects and for forging a shared vision for the achievement of the most critical goals.

- UNITY will thrive with the responsible leader's recognition and encouragement. Without this communication, UNITY dies.

- Everything is connected. One individual's decisions are likely to affect many other people. A team in a state of UNITY willingly engages in open supportive dialogue about *how* the various decisions and priorities affect everyone.

- UNITY can be recognized when you observe that:

  o People understand and respect each other's perspectives and processes.

  o They disengage from "battle mode", pacification, and wins and surrenders, and move to collaboration.

  o They know why systems are in place, but at the same time they don't mistake the systems for the mission.

  o They speak the same language regardless of what language they speak.

o They trust each other and are willing to hear each other out – because they know they are all working toward the same goals.

- There are lots of different tools you can use to spark and sustain the good communication that supports UNITY. Finding the right communication tools is an ongoing process, one that should never be considered "finished."

- UNITY allows you to adapt more rapidly and more effectively to shifts in the marketplace and/or to the changing needs of particular customers.

THE KEY QUESTIONS FOR PILLAR THREE

What is an example from your personal experience of a shared long-term goal, supported by a complementary vision, which united two different working groups? Take some time to think of the best example.

What made UNITY possible in your example?

What outside team (such as a vendor) might you create a state of UNITY with? What would be the best first step in doing that?

Where in your organization is UNITY across teams strongest? Why? And what benefit does this UNITY bring to your business?

Where in your organization could UNITY have the greatest possible impact? What first step would you suggest that could lead to bringing that improvement about?

Answer the questions above in writing. Once you've done that, consider sharing your responses with members of a peer group who can help you to identify the best follow-up questions ... and continue your organization's journey toward full Responsibility Culture.

THE FOURTH PILLAR:

Building Team Cohesion

Bringing a "one for all and all for one" approach to the workplace.

"The strength of the team is each individual member. The strength of each member is the team."

Phil Jackson, NBA Coach of the Year recipient

Isn't how people work together more important than how they work independently?

How much more effective could you and your organization be if you focused on leading and managing high performing *teams* ... rather than focusing individually on each person in your organization?

In this chapter, we examine the challenges and implications of real-world teambuilding for managers and entrepreneurs. For leaders, this means setting the vision – but it also means delegating and supporting the team as it moves forward toward its objective – and assuming personal responsibility for the outcomes of all those to whom responsibility has been delegated.

This kind of team-focused responsibility, demonstrated from the top down and built from the bottom up, is a powerful motivating force. We call it team cohesion. Making sure that cohesion happens consistently is one of the leader's most important responsibilities.

> The leader must make sure everyone knows that every meaningful victory belongs to the team and that each member of the team has a part to play in both securing the victory and in supporting Responsibility Culture.

George Patton's legendary speech to the Third Army in 1944, shortly before the D-Day invasion, is one of the most influential and important orations on the subject of team cohesion ever delivered. It's also a powerful reminder of the power of responsibility. In emphasizing the responsibility of the team, Patton quietly but persuasively reinforced his own *personal* responsibility for the results they delivered. That is the way it is with all great leaders. They know that when delegating responsibility for a task to someone who is ready to assume personal responsibility for executing it, the leader's own responsibility remains complete and undiminished.

Patton's remarks are regarded by many as the most successful and persuasive motivational speech of the 20th century. Note that his emphasis on "instant obedience to orders" and "constant alertness" connect, not to a desire to dominate for the sake of domination, but to the kind of team action that's instantaneous and almost automatic, without people having to stop and think about what their responsibility is – like a flock of birds moving together in flight. The most powerful excerpts (lightly edited to tone down the General's famously caustic tongue) appear below.

"You are not all going to die. Only two percent of you right here today would be killed in a major battle. Every man is scared in his first action. If he says he's not, he's a goddamn liar. But the real hero is the man who fights even though he's scared. Some men will get over their fright in a minute under fire, some take an hour, and for some it takes days. But the real man never lets his fear of death overpower his honor, his sense of duty to his country, and his innate manhood.

"All through your army career you men have bitched about what you call 'this pointless drilling.' That is all for a purpose—to ensure instant obedience to orders and to create constant alertness. This must be bred into every soldier. I don't give a damn for a man who is not always on his toes. But the drilling has made veterans of all you men. You are ready! A man has to be alert all the time if he expects to keep on breathing. If not, some German son-of-a-bitch will sneak up behind him and beat him to death. There are four hundred neatly marked graves in Sicily, all because one man went to sleep on the job—but they are German graves, because we caught the bastard asleep before his officer did.

"An army is a team. It lives, eats, sleeps, and fights as a team. This individual hero stuff is nonsense. The bastards who write that stuff for the Saturday Evening Post don't know anything about real battle. And we have the best team—we have the finest food

and equipment, the best spirit and the best men in the world. Why, by God, I actually pity these poor bastards we're going up against.

"All the real heroes are not storybook combat fighters. Every single man in the army plays a vital role. So, don't ever let up. Don't ever think that your job is unimportant. What if every truck driver decided that he didn't like the whine of the shells and turned yellow and jumped headlong into a ditch? That cowardly bastard could say to himself, 'Hell, they won't miss me, just one man in thousands.' What if every man said that? Where in the hell would we be then? No, thank God, Americans don't say that. Every man does his job. Every man is important. The ordnance men are needed to supply the guns. The quartermaster is needed to bring up the food and clothes for us because where we are going there isn't a hell of a lot to steal. Every last damn man in the mess hall, even the one who boils the water, has a job to do.

"Each man must think not only of himself, but think of his buddy fighting alongside him. One of the bravest men I saw in the African campaign was on a telegraph pole in the midst of furious fire while we were moving toward Tunis. I stopped and asked him what the hell he was doing up there. He answered, 'Fixing the wire, sir.' 'Isn't it a little unhealthy up there right now?' I asked. 'Yes sir, but this goddamn wire has got to be fixed.' I asked, 'Don't those planes strafing the road bother you?' And he answered, 'No sir, but you sure as hell do.' Now, there was a real soldier. A real man. A man who devoted all he had to his duty, no

matter how great the odds, no matter how seemingly insignificant his duty appeared at the time.

"And you should have seen the trucks on the road to Gabès. Those drivers were magnificent. All day and all night they crawled along those son-of-a-bitch roads, never stopping, never deviating from their course with shells bursting all around them. Many of the men drove over 40 consecutive hours. We got through on good old American guts. These were not combat men. But they were soldiers with a job to do. They were part of a team. Without them the fight would have been lost."

Patton got it absolutely right. Everyone has a part to play. No triumph belongs to one person. The team has the ultimate responsibility. By acknowledging that fact, and celebrating it, Patton empowered his (huge) team to one of the greatest victories in human history.

Everyone has a contribution to make to the support of the team approach we call a Culture of Responsibility. The challenge of the Leader is to identify the contribution and create the working environment that consistently makes it a reality.

"Find the best people to whom you can delegate, and know their strengths and weaknesses. If you think you can do it better, delegate anyway and try as hard as you can to close that gap by giving your colleague or employee the right feedback. Then recognize and accept that just because someone does something a little differently than you would, that doesn't mean it's wrong. What counts is that your goals get accomplished at a sufficient level of quality."

Eli Broad, entrepreneur and philanthropist

EMPOWERING YOUR TEAM

Many, many managers have no idea what it means to delegate. Some managers cringe every time the word *delegate* is used, which suggests there's a disconnect. Delegating means getting your people to a point where they have been prepared to assume personal responsibility for executing something important … intuitively … as a matter of habit … and then, stepping back to let them succeed or fail, knowing that their success or failure is still your personal responsibility.

Allow us to share a story that concisely exemplifies, in a business setting, exactly what General Patton accomplished with his now-legendary team cohesion speech in a military setting.

A few years ago, a company we worked with called The Wall required coordinated logistical interaction between multiple job sites. Various materials needed to be transported to job sites in a timely manner for the teams to complete their jobs efficiently. There was a major challenge to deal with, though, because the materials teams needed were, all too often, not showing up at sites on time for them to complete their work. A limited sense of what this was like can be gathered from what Patton expressed about the importance of the work of the truck drivers on the road to Gabès in completing their team's mission. In this case, though, the "trucks" were late and the mission was suffering.

The company owner, Rick McCutcheon, called the relevant team leads together and did, essentially, the same thing General Patton did – but in far fewer and more restrained words.

One afternoon, Rick brought his team leads out to a pizza parlor after work and said in essence, "Okay, thanks for coming, everyone. Here's why we've gone out for pizza. I guess you all know we've got a problem with materials moving between job sites. Things aren't synchronized, and we have teams working at different sites who are having trouble fulfilling their targets because they aren't getting what they need when they need it. Now, I trust you all to figure out how to make this work. So, what I'd like to do is, first, everyone order some pizza. Second, I'm going to move over to another table – I've got some paperwork to do. Third, while I'm doing that, I'd like you guys to work on this for a half an hour or so as you enjoy the pizza. Then let me know what you come up with as a solution you can all recommend and support."

What effect do you think that had on the team?

It galvanized and motivated them, for two big reasons. First, they all knew what they were responsible for delivering and that they were capable of delivering it. (That was a function of recruiting and training.) Second, they didn't want to let their leader down. (That was a function of personal leadership.)

Forty minutes later, the pizza was all gone, and the team had a recommendation to make. They signaled Rick, who came back over to the main table, listened to what they had come up with, and said, "Okay, let's do it. You guys go ahead and implement this new approach." The team leads had decided how each of their teams could take on more responsibility for this critical function.

There are two things to notice here. First, each member of the team was personally responsible for his or her role in the task that had been delegated – finding a solution to the logistical problem. And second, just as important, the owner had never stopped being personally responsible for the results they delivered. That's the nature of being a leader.

This is real delegation in action. It is exactly what General Patton accomplished – by means of a much longer speech. But the essence was the same. Everyone knew what the team job was and what his or her individual job was. And the leader was still responsible for the result. And notice that Patton doesn't micromanage the guy who boils the water, just as Rick didn't micromanage the discussion about the best solution.

> *"Deciding what not to do is as important as deciding what to do."*
>
> Jessica Jackley, entrepreneur and speaker

BEYOND "MY WAY OR THE HIGHWAY"

Jack was the lead consultant in a firm that supported the health-care industry. He had grown his consulting firm from a "one-man show" to a twenty-employee operation with an impressive local reputation. This growth had taken place over a period of 15 years, largely on the strength of Jack's commanding personality. More recently, though, the practice had hit a plateau, and four years ago, Jack had set the goal of resuming the growth trend and setting the stage for his own eventual retirement. There were some obstacles to achieving this, though.

Like so many small business owners, Jack had created a growth plan for his company that was based largely on his personal strengths. Ultimately, though, these same strengths had become limiting factors to the further growth of the company. His strong focus on his objectives had manifested in a lack of support for an open, growing team spirit. A gap between Jack and the next level of the company had formed.

Jack's stated aim – which he shared with friends whose opinion he trusted – was to sell his consulting practice and either retire or move on to another kind of professional challenge. He was eager for a change. The practice he led had built up a solid reputation, and Jack's own expertise lay at the heart of that positive reputation. Yet he knew the practice had stopped growing, and he also knew there was no clear successor on the horizon to lead the practice. Both of these factors stood in the way of Jack's ideal exit strategy: Selling his 80% share in the practice to Marian, the associate who had worked with him closely for more than a decade, and who owned the other 20% of the firm.

"I can't possibly sell the practice to Marian if she isn't ready to lead the company," Jack told his friends. "And the problem is, I'm not sure she ever *will* be ready to lead the company. Unfortunately, without a clear growth track and a stronger management team, I don't think I can sell it to anyone else, either. I'm caught between a rock and a hard place, and the big problem is that Marian has put me here. She simply hasn't stepped up."

That was Jack's perspective, and as a successful businessman he was certainly entitled to it. Yet after extensive discussions with his friends, and a series of one-on-one sessions with a personal success coach, Jack came to examine another possibility: That he himself was standing in the way of Marian's professional development.

The coach helped Jack uncover a major challenge: he often took a "my way or the highway" approach to running his business. He was tough, confident, and deeply committed to direct, immediate action in support of his own strategic goals. He was also distrustful of any decisions he did not personally double-check, and he was most comfortable telling team members – including Marian – exactly what to do in any and every situation. This had led to a "top-down" culture within his organization, under which virtually nothing happened unless Jack had personally approved all the details. Put bluntly, Jack was a prisoner of his own desire for control – and so was Marian, who had been unable to emerge as a company leader in her own right, for the simple reason that she was constantly being second-guessed by Jack. This controlling attitude affected, not just Marian, but the entire company.

The real reason Marian had not been able to spread her wings as a leader was not that she "hadn't stepped up," it was that Jack had never truly delegated any authority to her, and he had not been willing to support her as she made important decisions on her own.

This wasn't the only uncomfortable lesson. The coach helped Jack to realize that there was a sense throughout the company that the organization's focus was "all about Jack." Most employees felt the sole purpose of the enterprise was to promote him as an individual and expand his financial well-being … at the expense of other team members. This was a colossal cultural and morale problem.

This problem, it transpired, had been festering for years, and it had taken a toll on the staff. When Jack learned that Marian and several other key people had seriously considered leaving the firm because of a perception that Jack would *never* support the personal and professional growth of his subordinates, Jack asked his success coach for help. "I need you to help me change a pattern that's holding my practice back," he said. "I need to learn how to delegate more effectively, and I need to prove to my people that there really is a management career path for them to follow."

It took some time – over a year, in fact – but with ongoing support, encouragement, and, yes, some healthy peer pressure from his friends, Jack was able to turn around the "clear-everything-with-me-first" management style. He found new ways to give Marian meaningful decision-making authority on more and more aspects of the practice's day-to-day operation. He allowed Marian to bring her own, very different, decision making process into play as she pursued strategic goals. Letting Marian "do it her way" didn't come easily, and it wasn't comfortable, but it did allow Jack to lead the company in a way he never had before. During this period, Jack learned the difficult lesson that *delegating authority for decisions means stepping back and supporting the people who make those decisions ...* while still being personally responsible for the performance of the company as a whole. As a result, Marian reveled in the opportunity to do what she'd been longing to do for years: take on more responsibility.

Jack gradually learned how to delegate and give others a chance to shine. He stopped reciting a "mantra" that he now realized was holding his company back: "I've always done it that way." As a result, Marian came into her own as a company leader. Jack eventually negotiated the sale of his share of the practice to Marian.

The firm is now on an upward growth curve, and its culture has been transformed from "top-down" and "clear it with the boss" to one best described as "everyone grows" and "everyone gets the chance to learn how to make his or her optimum contribution." Jack, for his part, has moved on to start a whole new (non-competing) business.

> *"I get by with a little help from my friends."*
>
> John Lennon and Paul McCartney

QUIANA STEPS UP

ProLink Solutions, a residential real estate appraisal firm, was a small organization that had been hit by a sudden, intense market demand. From one point of view this was a windfall; from another, it was a major developmental challenge.

Dori, the owner of the company, knew the ProLink Solutions staff and infrastructure was unable to keep up with the workload. As she had been doing since the day she took over the firm, she stepped into the gap and took on more responsibility. She found herself working an endless series of twelve- and fourteen-hour days. This led to high levels of stress, an unsustainable workload, and her decision to seek the guidance of a coach. She felt unprepared to own or run the company.

As a result of her regular participation in coaching sessions, Dori learned that there are three basic types of contributors on any team: LEADERS, MANAGERS, and DOERS. There's no value judgment connected to falling into any of these roles; success is a matter of finding out which of the three roles you perform best in and taking Responsibility for and maximizing your meaningful contributions through that role.

Dori's coach helped her to uncover two important realities about her own, and her company's, situation. First and foremost, Dori was both a DOER and a LEADER. She enjoyed property appraisal and got great personal satisfaction out of doing that face-to-face work herself. Second, she was not a MANAGER. She had, in her own words, "fallen into" ownership of the company and was not comfortable or effective in a project management role. Her coach urged her to look to other team members who could help her to fill that gap.

Dori didn't have to look far. Her long-time assistant, Quiana, had already taken on many management responsibilities within the firm. She had seen a void and assumed personal responsibility for filling it. To Dori's immense relief, Quiana agreed to take on even more responsibility, steadily expanding on the role of office manager she had already established. Quiana was ready, willing, and eager to take on additional responsibilities that aligned with her own sense of personal growth and development.

Both Dori and Quiana blossomed under the new arrangement, and the company thrived.

Support a Team Approach!

THE TAKEAWAYS: PILLAR FOUR

No meaningful victory belongs to just one person. Everyone has a part to play. Everyone has a contribution to make to support a Culture of Responsibility.

It is the leader's responsibility to support people who are eager to take on deeper levels of responsibility and to create a rising class of leaders-in-training.

If a leader is not supportive of someone who is ready and willing to take on greater responsibilities to support the team, that person may become frustrated and look for other opportunities.

The surest and most positive way for a company to grow and prosper is by developing a spirit of growth and development among all people, one by one, team by team. Supporting such a culture of growth enables people to accept progressively greater levels of responsibility – enhancing the leadership of the company at all levels.

Team members must feel that their leaders are acting in the best interest of the company and of all members of the team. They must never feel that any decisions made, or actions taken, are for economic gain at their expense.

Fresh unbiased perspectives from peers and company outsiders can often help a leader see how his/her methods may be limiting the company's growth.

Beware of anyone in the company who says, "This is the way we/I have always done it". Mistakenly embracing old ways can cause a company to miss out on new processes and systems and markets that would do a better job of supporting the vision.

As we stated in the Introduction, one of the most important Responsibilities of leaders and managers of companies is to create team cohesion throughout the organization. In the end, however it is the people of the company who must take on the Responsibility, building an environment of cohesion through their daily actions. In support of this, the leader must recognize the accomplishments of individuals and teams whenever possible.

Ensure that the people and teams get credit for wins. (Not the leader)

Be selective about bringing Responsible people into your organization by recruiting for Ability, Responsibility, and Connectivity.

Remove people who won't accept responsibility. They will weaken any Culture of Responsibility.

THE KEY QUESTIONS FOR PILLAR FOUR

To what degree do you trust your teams to independently produce results upon which the company success or failure might depend?

Do you know which of your team members have an interest, aptitude, and ability to take on greater roles and responsibilities?

What support or development do these employees need from you to achieve their desired growth?

Who is the single most promising "leader-in-training" on staff right now who does not hold a management position?

What steps should be taken, and by whom, within the next 30 days to ensure that this individual continues to work and grow at your organization?

Are there any roles that you are currently doing that, if turned over to someone else, would allow you to focus on more important issues?

Answer the questions above in writing. Once you've done that, consider sharing your responses with members of a peer group who can help you to identify the best follow-up questions ... and continue your organization's journey toward a full Responsibility Culture.

THE FIFTH PILLAR:

Constant, Never-Ending Improvement

Set a course for ongoing excellence on both the personal and the organizational level.

Good, better, best; Never let it rest; 'Til your good is better, and your better is best.

Quote popularly attributed to St. Jerome

How much stronger and more valuable could your business become if you could continually learn and improve based on the input of stakeholders who are dedicated to becoming the best?

Great leaders know that success is not a destination, but a direction. Great teams prove this, day in and day out, week in and week out, year in and year out.

Here's an example of this principle. In the spring of 1943, General George C. Marshall wanted to be named Supreme Commander of Operation Overlord, the massive Allied invasion of occupied France that he had spent over a year helping to plan and prepare for. Although Marshall did not openly lobby President Franklin D. Roosevelt for the position, he let a close associate know where his sentiments lay when he said, in private, "Any soldier would prefer a field command."

Marshall, already regarded as one of the greatest military minds of his generation, was willing to step down as Chief of Staff of the Army in order to take on the job of Supreme Commander ... if President Roosevelt offered the post to him. He was so widely seen as the favorite for this position that a subordinate (without Marshall's knowledge) jumped the gun in preparing for his seemingly inevitable appointment. The subordinate arranged for a special desk, matching Marshall's desk in Washington, to be sent overseas for his exclusive use during planning sessions for what was to be the largest sea-borne invasion in military history.

In the end, however, Roosevelt picked Dwight D. Eisenhower to lead Operation Overlord, telling Marshall, "I didn't feel I could sleep at ease if you were out of Washington." Marshall accepted the President's decision and continued to fulfill his responsibilities stateside, staying on with the Joint Chiefs of Staff. He brought his extraordinary skills as a planner, motivator, and strategist to the task of coordinating the extensive US military campaigns that were underway in Europe and the Pacific.

And he kept moving forward.

If General Marshall had any remorse or regret over having failed to secure the historic position he desired, he did not show it to anyone. Asked once about the various obstacles and disappointments he had faced during the course of his career, Marshall said, "When a thing is done, it's done. Don't look back. Look forward to your next objective."

On another occasion, Marshall observed that "what other people do shouldn't affect you. We do things because of the kind of people we want to be."

Marshall followed these two principles closely in carrying out what he was responsible for carrying out. He fulfilled his duty to the President and to the country, and he did so at such a high level of excellence that Winston Churchill referred to him as "the true organizer of Allied victory." (It is worth noting in passing that Eisenhower, who led Operation Overlord and was later elected President of the United States, not only followed Marshall's strategic lead in executing the D-Day invasion, but was himself a Marshall protege.)

General Marshall was always looking forward to his next objective. And he was always doing things because of the kind of person he wanted to be, not because of external influences or short-term expediencies. In contemporary terminology, we would say, Marshall qualified as a proponent of the principle of **Constant, Never-Ending Improvement:** excellence at a rising level and for its own sake.

Nowhere was his ongoing commitment to excellence for its own sake more evident than in the selection of Marshall, in 1953, as the recipient of the Nobel Peace Prize. Eight years after the victorious conclusion of the cataclysmic war he had been called upon to end, Marshall received humankind's foremost honor for the pursuit of peace. He won largely because of his leadership (as Secretary of State) in the successful, and historically unprecedented, campaign to rebuild a war-shattered Europe.

The formal name of that campaign was the Marshall Plan, and Marshall was its architect. Simply put, the plan put America's money where its mouth was.

From 1948 to 1952, the Marshall Plan pumped over $13 billion of American funds (roughly $180 billion today) into shattered Western European economies. The initiative not only stopped Communism from spreading into nations like France and Great Britain, but it also cemented a Western alliance of democratic, market-focused nations that laid the groundwork for the security of the entire postwar era. (Eastern European nations were invited to take part in the Marshall Plan, but were forbidden to do so by Soviet authorities.)

The Marshall Plan was an achievement of truly historic proportions – and it only came about because General George C. Marshall knew that the United States in general, and he in particular, were responsible for establishing a sound foundation for peace following the devastation of World War II. Marshall knew from personal experience that success is a direction, not a stopping point. He knew that true responsibility does not stop at a given point, even after the achievement of a goal as momentous as victory in the Second World War. He knew that America, at its deepest level, was and is about aspiration, about continuous improvement. And he put that knowledge into daily practice for the benefit, not only of his country, but of all humanity. That's what won him the Nobel Peace Prize.

"We must stop setting our sights," Marshall once observed, "by the light of each passing ship. Instead, we must set our course by the stars." This is the final, and we believe the highest, management responsibility: creating and sustaining an organizational culture that is committed, as Marshall was, to continuous, ongoing, improvement. In his lifetime, that impulse to "set our course by the stars" led to a rebirth of opportunity, and to a foothold for democracy, in Western Europe. It arose in a time of great darkness. In our time, we should ask ourselves: What darkness faces us most oppressively? And what star within that darkness is waiting to guide us as we set our course?

THE VAST RESPONSIBILITY

"A very serious situation is rapidly developing which bodes no good for the world. The modern system of the division of labor upon which the exchange of products is based is in danger of breaking down. The truth of the matter is that Europe's requirements for the next three or four years of foreign food and other essential product – principally from America – are so much greater than her present ability to pay that she must have substantial additional help, or face economic, social, and political deterioration of a very grave character.... It would be neither fitting nor efficacious for this Government to undertake to draw up unilaterally a program designed to place Europe on its feet economically. This is the business of the Europeans. The initiative, I think, must come from Europe. The role of this country should consist of friendly aid in the drafting of a European program and of later support of such a program so far as it may be practical for us to do so. The program should be a joint one, agreed to by a number, if not all, of European nations. An essential part of any successful action on the part of the United States is an understanding on the part of the people of America of the character of the problem and the remedies to be applied. Political passion and prejudice should have no part. With foresight, and a willingness on the part of our people to face up to the vast responsibility which history has clearly placed upon our country, the difficulties I have outlined can and will be overcome."

General George C. Marshall, June 5, 1947

ON BECOMING THE BEST

When Mike started coaching business owners, he began with the processes that they should follow to be successful. While this coaching was reasonably effective, he realized something that went back to the Air Defense Artillery battery in Korea, and even farther back, to Saint Jerome's admonition "Good, Better, Best; Never let it Rest." Mike realized that the question that had to be asked of each leader was, "What are you currently the best at … or becoming the best at?"

In all Mike's future coaching sessions, the leaders and their people had to know … and buy into … the company's answer to this question. They had to know where they were and where they were going. The transformation was remarkable. This question changed how people spoke, acted, reacted, and performed. It changed the confidence people had in their cultures. Those who most clearly answered this question found that success came more easily and that their people became prouder, more effective, and more willing to take on Responsibility. Knowing what they were best at or becoming the best at made it easier for people to explain their value to customers. And what customer doesn't want to know they are getting the best … and then to tell others about it? This question became a positive driving force in the culture that drove Mike's coaching clients to continually strive to retain and extend their marketplace position.

The rate of improvement for those companies that focused on their vision of being the best was striking. Some began achieving significant growth during the heart of the Great Recession – all because they went from thinking about surviving to thinking about thriving.

IF YOU REALLY WANT TO IMPROVE SOMETHING – ASK YOURSELF: CAN YOU MEASURE IT?

Perhaps you're wondering: What does this outlook – the outlook of becoming the best, of moving forward, of creating something new and better, of building something better and beyond the scale of anything previously attempted – look like in a practical business context?

It starts with metrics. Consider the case of Earle Bevins, founder of The Global Display Solution, who was one of Phil's first TAB Board members. (You'll find out more about TAB Boards in the epilogue of this book.) Over nearly a decade, his company has grown fourfold. That's a really dramatic growth record. One of the biggest drivers behind this dramatic growth record is Earle's personal commitment to constant, never-ending improvement. In his case, it's a commitment to excellence that's rooted in a pervasive organizational focus on Key Performance Indicators (KPIs).

For every functional area of the company, Earle has a set of KPIs that he and responsible employees monitor and update every month. There are dozens of them, all visible to those people responsible for the company's achievements on a series of graphs. The graphs function like the dashboard of an automobile, alerting the "driver", Earle or his team, about all the relevant performance levels and potential warning signs. If you're about to run out of gas, your car sends you a warning while there's still time to find a service station. It's the same thing with Earle's graphs: they're designed to get him the critical information he needs about each operational area, so that he and his team members can focus on supporting the most critical improvements.

The effective visual display of information is important to any leader's attempt to sustain a culture of constant, never-ending improvement. Being able to see the metrics, in ways that engage the viewer, drives commitment to key initiatives throughout the organization. In Earle's case, he uses the visual data constantly in working with multiple teams to develop and refine the processes and procedures that generate all that monthly-updated data.

The KPI metrics Earle monitors include:

- Quotes sent out, and the percentage that turn into business. (This is part of the sales team's KPI metric set. There are many other metrics also.)

- Inventory management metrics. (For instance, the number of times the company is unable to ship because of insufficient inventory. There's an ongoing balancing act between keeping customers happy and not overloading the company's warehouses with inventory. It's worth noting that Earle's company is importing finished goods and does not operate in a manufacturing environment. If they did, there would be a different set of KPIs to track.)

- Web visits.

- Web sales.

- Accuracy of order entry, invoicing, and fulfillment. (A particularly important issue is: how many errors are entered into the system, and how do we nudge that number closer to zero?)

Earle and his team are constantly monitoring all of this. They have to. If you can't measure it, how can you possibly know whether or not you're improving it? By the way, let's pause to point out that General Marshall took exactly the same approach in implementing the Marshall Plan. He made sure that its disbursements were keyed to specific economic objectives within a given country taking part in the program; constant ongoing measurements against those objectives were a central component of the Economic Cooperation Authority (ECA) that administered the aid. The writer Michael J. Hogan noted that the program's metrics were carefully tracked – and that the results were dramatic. ECA figures confirmed that "Western Europe's aggregate gross national product jumped by more than 32 percent, from $120,000 million to $159,000 million. Agricultural production climbed 11 percent above the prewar level, and industrial output increased by 40 percent against the same benchmark."

We should go back to Earle. Thanks to his tireless efforts, his company has built up a similarly rigorous culture of measurement and analysis. In fact, KPI evaluation has become a central component of his personal growth plan for the business, which involves making the company more and more self-sufficient – extracting his personal oversight of individual processes and handing off more and more responsibility to individual team members ready, willing and eager to accept it. In every aspect of the business, this is the plan. Commitment to constant never-ending improvement leads to larger and larger zones of personal responsibility for specific initiatives within the enterprise … and smaller and smaller zones of potential overload and stress for the company founder.

What those KPIs are doing is *clarifying everyone's responsibility*. Each and every visual expression of a particular metric on Earle's whiteboard reflects a clear zone of responsibility, undertaken both individually and as a team. **In an organization committed to constant, never-ending improvement, KPIs always connect to specific responsibilities, and specific opportunities for both delegation and personal growth.** That means coaching, communication, and giving people the authority to try things and make mistakes. (Of course, a big part of Earle's job is ensuring that the zones within which his people are granted the right to make mistakes are areas that won't cause catastrophic setbacks to the business.)

KPIs should be a visible tool you use to tie past performance to present-tense commitments that affect the future of your business. They should be an entry-point to a clear discussion about the direction, the new benchmarks being set, and the acceptance of public responsibility for reaching those benchmarks. That's how Earle uses them, as a starting point for a discussion about who's making a commitment to do what and by when – so as to bring about a particular, measurable, targeted improvement.

Use a discussion about visually represented KPIs, delivered via a dashboard display system, such as TAB's Business Builder Blueprint, to ensure that there is publicly assumed individual and team responsibility for specific measurable improvements. These improvements should be targeted to take place by a specific date. Work with people and coach them, both individually and in a team setting, based on the particular KPI they've assumed as a personal and team responsibility. This is a core principle of all organizations that manage to build constant, never-ending improvement into their working culture.

LITTLE CHANGES

Big improvements are sometimes necessary, as the Marshall Plan example shows. Big changes are very costly, though, and they often carry major growth implications for the enterprise. The most vulnerable time for a company is when it's in a state of major change. Fortunately, big changes are not the only way to implement a culture of continuous improvement. The business philosophy of constant, never-ending improvement is often referred to by a Japanese name, "Kaizen." This Japanese word translates simply as "change for better" and can refer to either large or small improvements.

Among the most popular and productive applications of the Kaizen principle is that of adopting a continuous openness to minor, easy-to-implement, and typically inexpensive improvements in team process, in individual performance, or in both areas. Over time, these seemingly minor improvements can have a dramatic, positive cumulative impact on an organization's competitive position. Constant low-level changes present a much more attractive risk picture ... and they can still get you great results, because they don't require all groups within the organization to adapt to change at the same time.

> Set up a program that recognizes and rewards team members for identifying specific areas where there is something that can be improved – and tested it in small area – before rolling the change out to the organization as a whole.

A company Mike worked with, HCO, referenced elsewhere in this book, regularly rewarded employees at all levels for taking part in a process which has since become known as "piddle, diddle, and fiddle." This is a fanciful way of expressing the decision to reward employees for examining their own team's processes to find instances of inefficiency, redundancy, and overlap. In essence, the leader gave his people permission to ask a powerful question: "Why do we do it that way?"

Once people spotted something that didn't add value, they could change it in their own team, on their own authority ... and share their discovery with the rest of the company. This culture of constant experimentation in the pursuit of minor improvements actually led to a major breakthrough. Tasked with finding out why certain parts were failing at a high rate due to excessive moisture, one of the teams followed the "piddle, diddle, and fiddle" approach to identify steps or activities that are superfluous to the manufacturing process.

The team members took a close look at the production line that delivered the parts – and found a step where there was a water wash of circuits. A question arose: Why are we washing the circuits with water?

It seemed like a pretty simple question, but the team's engineers couldn't answer it. Finally, someone found an employee who had been working on the production line for a long time and asked the same question: Why are we doing it this way?

The answer was simple. Force of habit. At one time, the company had to get rid of water-soluble flux that built up on the circuits during soldering – but that was years ago. HCO no longer made the circuits that way, and washing with water was no longer necessary. They now had a flux-less soldering process.

The "fiddle, diddle, and piddle" mindset led to a simple fix that dramatically reduced failure rates on the production line. Because they were willing to ask, "Why do we do it that way?", the employees were able to eliminate a step that was no longer relevant and was, in fact, lowering quality.

The moral here is a powerful one. Recognize and reward your team members for spotting little things that, when remedied or redesigned or removed, offer the possibility of small-scale positive changes. Encourage them to put a little extra effort into identifying places where they may be doing something they don't need to do – or not doing something they need to do. Recognize and compensate them when they spot opportunities for (seemingly) tiny improvements. You'll be surprised what kinds of improvements in efficiency you can generate by freeing people up to work as a team in recognizing and taking out minor inefficiencies.

SUCCESS IS A DIRECTION, NOT A STOPPING POINT

What does it mean to embrace constant, never-ending improvement as a way of doing business – and a way of living life?

It means doing what General Marshall did: Moving forward, even after a setback, to create a new direction of possibility and constant improvement in your life, to the benefit of others. By the same token, it means continuously moving forward, even after you've attained something important for yourself and the team.

It means setting a new target when conditions change. If you're 80% of the way toward hitting the sales goal, and you're only halfway through the second quarter, guess what? It's time to set the bar a little higher.

It means embracing the idea of constantly reorienting yourself, your team, and your organization toward "true north." You're never going to get to "true north," but you're going to head in that direction.

It means stating what your current conception of perfection is, in measurable terms, so you can assume personal responsibility for moving toward it.

It means not getting discouraged because you don't reach perfection. It means remembering that setting impossible standards for yourself and others can be demotivating.

It means celebrating benchmark victories. It means motivating people by rewarding them for making progress *toward* perfection – not withholding recognition and reward until they're perfect!

It means remembering that benchmarks are different from goals. Benchmarks are measure of progress toward perfection, and that's what you need to celebrate. Don't limit your focus to short term goals. The things that got you to the goal are not the things that will get you to the next level of Responsible contribution. Instead of setting a "team goal" or an "individual goal," set a benchmark that is aligned with the North Star – one that's realistic, but a bit of a stretch. Focus on the stretch benchmark, and see how close you can come to attaining it by a given point in time. You can recognize improvement toward your ultimate state and possibly refocus as things change. Notice how different this is from the demotivating possibility of "setting a goal," which just about everyone dreads the process of achieving – e.g., "My goal was to lose twenty pounds. Then if you do achieve it, you are at risk of gaining it back. That back and forth cycle doesn't help anyone.

Goals are aides to help those of us who haven't yet developed the ability to keep focused on the desired vision or have not yet developed that ability.

Finally, success means remembering that **you are personally responsible for your own self-improvement and your own growth and development.** That's the foundation of your responsibility to your team members, your customers, and all the other people you serve.

True story: Teddy Roosevelt – our 26th President – was an American statesman, author, explorer, soldier, officer, naturalist, reformer – and above all, a leader. On the morning of his death, January 6, 1919, his family found, beneath his pillow, a book on leadership. Gravely ill, he had been reading it before he fell asleep the night before. Even as he approached his final hours, Roosevelt was constantly focusing on the question, "How can I improve?"

Let's resolve to follow Roosevelt's example. We'll share some final thoughts on how you can best do that, for yourself and your organization, in the Epilogue.

Commit to Constant, Never-Ending Improvement!

THE TAKEAWAYS: PILLAR FIVE

Success is a direction, not a destination. The best leaders set a course for ongoing growth and development at the individual level, at the team level, and for the organization as a whole.

Seek to be the best. Your perspective changes once you define what the best looks like in whatever you do. It is what you dedicate yourself to becoming and remaining.

To improve anything, you must first know, "How will we measure it?"

Use Key Performance Indicators (KPIs) to maintain a pervasive organizational focus, and provide an alert while there's still time to take action to stay on course, like the gas gage of your car.

Responsible people must define, monitor, and update KPIs regularly to guide and stretch each functional area of the organization in light of current performance.

In an organization committed to constant, never-ending improvement, KPIs always connect to and clarify specific responsibilities by tying past performance to present and future commitments.

Dashboards, charts, or other visual displays show progress toward important benchmarks. The visual display of information is an effective communication tool for attaining and sustaining a culture of constant, never-ending improvement.

Sometimes big changes are necessary to achieve significant improvement, but in business, as in many sports, many little moves effectively set up big plays that enable you to get higher rewards at lower risk.

The business philosophy of constant, never-ending improvement is often referred to by a Japanese name, "Kaizen." This Japanese word translates simply as "change for better" and can refer to either large or small improvements.

Constant low-level positive changes can get you faster results more safely, because they don't require all groups within the organization to change at the same time.

A program that recognizes and rewards teams for identifying specific areas for improvement – and is tested under controlled conditions will spawn many more improvements.

Benchmarks and goals each have their purpose. Remember that Benchmarks are measures of progress toward perfection … and need to be celebrated!

The leader is personally responsible for his/her own self-improvement and personal growth and development, which is foundational to that of your team members, your customers, and all the other people you serve.

THE KEY QUESTIONS FOR PILLAR FIVE

- How would you describe your employees' current level of motivation? (For instance: "They are motivated to make our company the best," or perhaps "They are motivated to get through the day and get by.")

- What do you think your best customers would say or do differently if they were convinced that you were constantly working to offer them better products and services?

- In a worst-case scenario, how long do you think it would take for you to be overtaken by your closest competitor in your most valuable account?

- What specific, measurable future performance goals have you discussed with your team?

- What THREE Key Performance Indicators would have the greatest impact on the pursuit of your company's vision if they were measured and analyzed regularly?

- Who would be the ideal person to set up (or improve) a visual display system that would display recent performance levels for each of these Key Performance Indicators?

- As of now, how are team members rewarded for identifying specific areas where there is something in the organization that can be improved?

- How *should* they be rewarded?

Answer the questions above in writing. Once you've done that, consider sharing your responses with members of a peer group who can help you to identify the best follow-up questions ... and continue your organization's journey toward full Responsibility Culture.

EPILOGUE:

What's Next?

We believe that truly great leadership in any field and any culture means being able to select and enlist Responsible people to attain the best possible results from them by leading Responsibly ... and by inspiring them to follow your example. In this book, we've shared the five critical elements that support building this culture of personal Responsibility on any team:

- *The First Pillar: Answering the Question, "Why Are We Here?"*

- *The Second Pillar: Gaining Enrollment through Shared Values*

- *The Third Pillar: Creating UNITY to Achieve Long-Term Success ... Together*

- *The Fourth Pillar: Building Team Cohesion*

- *The Fifth Pillar: Constant, Never-Ending Improvement*

We hope what we've shared has been helpful ... and we want to challenge you to go beyond a hypothetical understanding of Responsibility, into a state of *action*. We want you to begin infusing Responsibility into the culture of your organization in the manner that is best suited to your unique situation. Our examples should give you and your team a starting point for finding your organization's way of encouraging and supporting a culture of Responsibility. As you do so, we invite you to share your experiences with other leaders by visiting us at responsibility-culture.com and consider sharing your experiences and support with other leaders through groups like the ones we have had the opportunity to lead over the last ten years through TAB Boards International.

TAB Boards International is a global network that offers business owners / senior leaders an opportunity to share valuable collective wisdom and real-world advice with their peers and experienced professional coaches who are armed with a process to achieve greater personal and business success.

TAB's Business Owner Advisory Boards provide something that many people at the top of their organizations find they don't get in any other way: a commitment to their peers to take action and achieve important objectives for their organizations that they have pledged personal Responsibility for achieving. Leaders achieve a greater focus and clarity that aligns their company with their vision for the business success and achieve a culture that benefits all. They benefit from an ongoing process that requires patience, guidance, and support. Perhaps most important, we have observed TAB members' attitudes benefit from sharing their accomplishments, challenges, lessons, commitments, and aspirations … and reminding each other of the steps they've committed to take toward the goal of supporting and fulfilling the Responsibility Culture you've read about in this book.

You can learn more about our TAB groups by visiting us at http://www.tab-pdxwest.com/